# Physical Characte
# Irish Red and W
## (from The Kennel Club

**Body:** Strong and muscular, deep chest and well sprung ribs. Back and quarters very muscular and powerful. Bone strong, well built up with muscle and sinew.

**Tail:** Strong at root, tapering to fine point; with no appearance of ropiness, not reaching below hock. Well feathered, carried level with back or below in lively manner.

**Coat:** Finely textured with good feathering. Slight wave permissible but never curly.

**Hindquarters:** Wide and powerful. Legs from hip to hock long and muscular from hock to heel short and strong. Stifle well bent, hocks well let down turning neither in nor out.

**Size:** Desirable height at withers: dogs 62.2–66 cms (24.5 inches); bitches 57.2–61 cms (22.5–24 inches).

**Feet:** Close-knit, well feathered between toes.

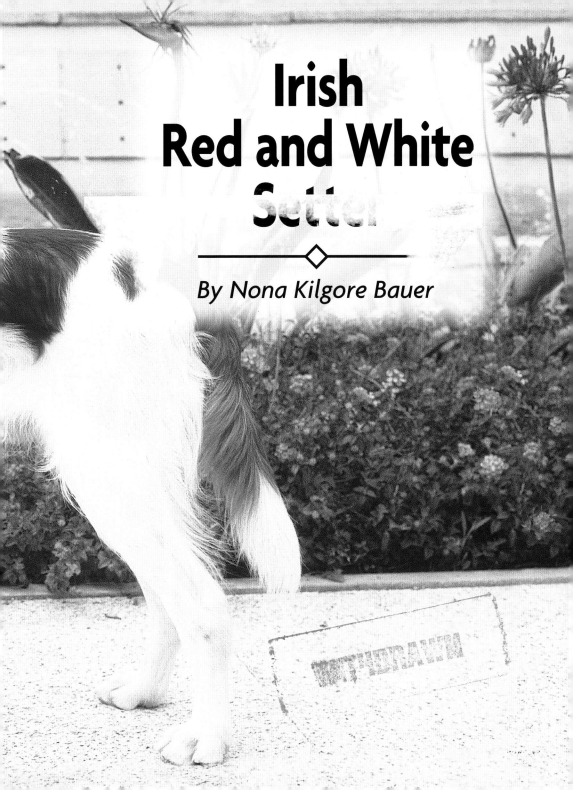

# Irish
# Red and White
# Setter

*By Nona Kilgore Bauer*

# Contents

Copyright © 2003 Kennel Club Books, Inc. Allenhurst, NJ 07711 USA Printed in South Korea.

PUBLISHED IN THE UNITED KINGDOM BY:

**INTERPET**
PUBLISHING

Vincent Lane, Dorking, Surrey RH4 3YX England

ISBN 1-84286-021-6

Photography by Carol Ann Johnson and Michael Trafford, with additional photographs by:

Norvia Behling, TJ Calhoun, Carolina Biological Supply, Doskocil, Isabelle Francais, James Hayden-Yoav, James R Hayden, RBP, Bill Jonas, Dwight R Kuhn, Dr Dennis Kunkel, Mikki Pet Products, Phototake, Jean Claude Revy, Dr Andrew Spielman and Alice van Kempen.

**Illustrations by Patricia Peters.**

The publisher would like to thank all of the owners of the dogs featured in this book, including Margaret Adamson, Graham & Jacqueline Bayne, Pedro Ferrao Completo, Thomas Hoevener, June Hill and Carol Pike; special thanks to Leanne Lindsay and Martyn Wilson.

The Irish Red and White Setter was treasured for several centuries by a small cadre of devoted dog fanciers; the breed became recognised by the dog world in more recent times.

# History of the
# IRISH RED AND WHITE SETTER

The history of Ireland is filled with myths, legends and, of course, the famous leprechaun. Less known, but no less revered, is Ireland's signature hunting and companion dog, the elegant and brilliant Irish Red and White Setter. The ancestor of its better known descendant, the red Irish Setter, the Red and White reigns strong in many an Irish dog owner's heart.

Although his genetic history is closely tied to his red Irish Setter relative, and he is equally distinct in coat and carriage, the Red and White has left his own unique pawprint on the Irish landscape. Adorned with a pearly white coat marked with deep chestnut patches, his muzzle gently splashed with the red freckles reminiscent of an Irish urchin, the Red and White is firmly entrenched as a companion gundog in both Ireland and Great Britain.

For several centuries, the Irish Red and White Setter roamed the knobby hills of Ireland, recognised as a superior hunting dog and treasured by a small cadre of devoted Irish breeders who worked diligently to preserve the breed. Because most breeding practices of that long-ago era were personal ventures and, for the most part, undocumented, much of what is known about this lively sporting dog dates back to the generic canine hunter that is the ancestor of all hunting breeds.

The first setter breeds are believed to date back to the original spaniel, the common term then used to describe any sporting dog. The spaniel [or 'spanyell,' as it was called during the era of Henry VIII (1491–1547), King of

*Charm, beauty and red hair runs through many Irish families, and the Irish Red and White Setter is no exception to those virtues.*

England and Ireland] takes its name from its country of origin, Spain, which is considered by most historians to be the homeland of the hunting dog that later found its way to England, Ireland and France. Although it is not clear exactly when the Irish Red and White Setter appeared on the scene, breed historians have found mention of an Irish Spaniel in *The Laws of Howell*, an antiquated tome written before the 11th century. Early canine literature also contains other references to 'Spaniels, mostly white with red patches' during the 14th century.

One must first understand the use of the early sporting breeds to fully appreciate the working nature of the modern-era spaniel and setter. Prior to the invention and use of firearms, the hunting spaniel was the only method of

Most historians believe that the red Irish Setter and the Irish Red and White Setter have co-existed as hunting dogs in Ireland for the past three centuries.

procuring food-source birds for the dinner table. The dogs worked in tandem with their owners—the dogs were sent forth to find and disturb the birds; the owner then released trained hawks and falcons to catch the birds as they flew off to make their escape.

The use of falcons eventually fell from favour, and the hunter turned to netting as the preferred method used in bird work. Paintings and references from 16th-century literature offer vivid

The red Irish Setter, closely linked to the more colourful subject of this book, remains the more popular of the two breeds, recognised by every major dog-registering organisation in the world.

descriptions of the hunting canine known as the 'netting dog.' When the netting dog had located the bird or covey of birds, he posed stiffly with one foreleg raised and 'set,' pointing to the exact location of the birds. On his master's command, he would drop to his belly and crawl closer to his prey, at which point the hunter would throw the net over his feathered quarry to capture the bird.

Perhaps the best-known historical reference to this setter behaviour is found in the famed *De Canibus Britannicus*, a 1570 work by Dr John Caius. Here we find mention of a 'Setter' who remains 'silent and sure...making no noise either with foote or with tongue...' Upon finding the birds, he then 'layeth his belly to the ground and so creepeth forward like a worme. When he approached neere to the place where the birde is, he layes him downe, and with marcke of his pawes, betrayeth the place of the byrdes last abode...' The 'marcke,' of course, refers to the signature raised foreleg of the setter breeds.

The setter is recognised again in the 1616 publication *The Country Farmer*, which describes 'another sort of land spannyels which are called setters.' It is assumed by most dog experts that the dog's creeping behaviour was trained or induced by man, although that is not confirmed in any literature. Later, in the 1726

*Treatise on Field Diversion*, we read of two distinct tribes of setters: 'the black and tanned, and the orange, lemon and white.'

During that distant time, there were no established breeds of dog. Dogs were valued for their usefulness and working talents, and dogs that demonstrated good working ability were bred to other dogs of like quality in hopes of producing another generation of good working stock. The conformation of any particular dog used was not a concern in most circumstances. Thus, it is quite amazing that today's setters so closely resemble those depicted in 18th-century artwork. In fact, the 1850 writings of H D Richardson describe the Irish Setter as the one setting breed least interfered with by the common breeding experiments of the time. 'No trace of the Pointer was seen in him. These are genuine unmixed descendants of the original land spaniel. This is a dog of very high esteem.'

By the early 17th century, setting dogs had been established as a recognisable type of sporting dog. Many authorities believe that the all-red dogs originally came from breeding red and white dogs that had increasing amounts of red. A study of Dr Caius' notes seems to indicate that selective breeding from white and red to predominantly red was already afoot in the 16th century. He writes, 'The most part of their skyness are white, and if they are marked with any spottes, they are commonly red, and somewhat great therewithall.' All varieties of colour were accepted at that time, and a wide colour variance existed among the breeders, so it is impossible to determine exactly when the all-red setter appeared.

By the late 1700s, several varieties of red and white setter had been well established by several prominent kennels that were producing their own strains. Travel between the different regions of Ireland was arduous, so it was no surprise that distinct varieties of the breed developed in certain areas of the country. All, however, carried some version of the red and white coat, with some predominantly white setters showing but a few red patches, some bearing the legendary 'shower of hail' colouring and others showing large blankets of colour across the back. Even the slightest trace of black hair was prohibited and, even today, purists maintain that any black hair on an Irish Setter means that it is not pure-bred.

During the mid-18th century in Ireland, the best dogs were to be found on the estates of wealthy sportsmen, as only the very rich could afford to keep and breed large numbers of dogs for pleasure sports such as shooting birds. These dogs were the prized possessions of their owners, being fleet of foot and possessing the stamina necessary to work on Ireland's rough terrain. Thus, the development of any specific breed of dog lay in the hands of a privileged few. It is believed that the red Irish Setter and the Irish Red and White Setter co-existed peacefully for most of the last three centuries, with little prefer-ence being shown for one colour over the other; in fact, many well-known breeders owned, worked and hunted over both reds and red and whites.

Once the Irish Red and White Setter began appearing at dog shows, coat colour became an issue of great importance among breeders and exhibitors. While many of the dog shows offered separate classes for the all-red Irish Setter and the Red and Whites, others declared that they could be shown together. There was much confusion as to the proper colour of the breed; some dogs had patches of white in their coats while others showed traces of black, which is a major flaw in the Irish setter breeds.

The founding of the Irish Red Setter Club in 1882 was so successful in promoting the red variety of Irish Setter that the Red and White numbers suffered greatly during the latter part of the 19th century. By the late 1800s, the red Irish Setter had eclipsed the Red and White, which

## HUTCHINSON'S BOB

The famous red Irish Setter, Hutchinson's Bob, is allegedly a descendant of a famous line of Red and Whites bred by Miss Lidwell during the early 19th century. Miss Lidwell's dogs can be found in the pedigrees of many modern Setters.

diminished the breed's popularity to the point where some believed it to be extinct.

The true revival of the Red and White began decades later in the post-war era of the 1920s. World War I had wrought great hardship on the people of Ireland and their dogs. The war had decimated the canine population in most countries, and many breeders and fanciers were forced to give up or euthanise their beloved animals. No exception, the Irish Red and White Setter, already disastrously low in numbers, almost disappeared.

Determined to persevere during that difficult time, several prominent Irish Red and White Setter fanciers set about restoring the breed as shooting dogs. Most notable among those responsible for the resurgence of the breed is the Reverend Noble Houston, a clergyman from Ballynahinch in County Down. Rev. Houston was joined in his venture by his cousin, Dr Elliott. Dr Elliott lived in a house named Eldron, a name that

was destined to become the prefix for their line of dogs. The two gentlemen obtained a bitch named Gyp, who was out of a red bitch and sired by a red and white dog. Rev. Houston bred Gyp to a setter named Johnnie, a mating that produced the foundation stock for the modern Irish Red and White Setter. Through selective breeding, he went on to build a kennel of Red and Whites. Houston's Bobs of Derryboy went on to win the All Ireland Challenge Cup at Haselmere in 1926. Bobs is prominent in many of today's pedigrees.

The Rev. Houston was determined to preserve the

Since the end of the 19th century, the modern red Irish Setter has outnumbered the Red and White Setter dramatically.

working ability of his dogs, and he took great care to emphasise working qualities when using any dog in his breeding programme. He further encouraged others to do likewise. In his later years, he carried on a lengthy correspondence with Mrs Maureen Cuddy, a fellow fancier from Midelton, County Cork, who shared a deep love for the Irish Red and White Setter. He frequently advised her to be sure she bred for work and not merely for the bench.

Rev. Houston did not keep official or formal pedigrees of his breeding efforts. He instead kept his records in his parish register, documenting various matings and whelpings, his own as well as others that he had researched from as far back as the late 1700s. When Rev. Houston passed away, Mrs Cuddy's husband, Mr William Cuddy, went to the parish register and carefully copied all those breeding records in order to preserve them for future generations. The Cuddys' efforts in compiling Rev. Houston's records created an invaluable historical profile of how the present-day Irish Red and White Setter came to be.

Mrs Cuddy's passion for the breed had begun in 1940 when she was given a sickly Red and White pup to nurse back to health. Under her tender hand, the pup survived, and indeed thrived, and Mrs Cuddy named

her Judith Cunningham of Knockalla. Although the dog was bred only once, to Jack of Glenmaquin, it is believed that every registered Red and White is descended from this bitch.

By 1944, breed numbers were still somewhat limited, but the Red and White had become well enough established to warrant its own breed club, the Irish Red and White Setter Society. The Cuddys were pivotal figures in the formation of the club and in drawing up the following stated objectives of the organisation:

1. To encourage the working qualities of the breed in every possible way.

2. To promote the breeding of them upon sound working principles.

3. To ensure that if they were classified at shows, they were judged from a working standpoint.

Mr and Mrs Cuddy continued to be an important link in the further development of the Red and White. Over the next three decades, they continued to breed the Knockalla Red and Whites, always keeping accurate records and registering their whelp and breeding stock.

In 1974, Mrs Cuddy was also a key element in convincing the Irish Kennel Club (IKC) to accept then-unregistered dogs into their ranks, which thus provided a vital link to the survival of the breed. The IKC in 1970 had halted

## REVIVAL ATTEMPT

In 1945, Mrs E F James of Rutland, England, became interested in the Irish Red and White Setter and attempted to revive the breed in England. She imported litter sisters, Constance of Knockalla and Colleen Bawn of Knockalla, and, after showing them several times, sent them back to Ireland for breeding. However, her efforts were unsuccessful and the resulting puppies fell into oblivion, fading during a time when unregistered stock was prevalent.

further registration of Red and Whites until it could be proven that no English Setter blood had been introduced into the breed. Thanks to her penchant for keeping precise records of her own and other breedings and whelpings, and her work in preserving Rev. Houston's records, Mrs Cuddy literally held the future of the Irish Red and White Setter in her hands. She submitted a lengthy statement of breedings dating back to 1953, naming dogs and breeders, in an effort to prove that the breed was pure Irish and had not been tainted by crosses with the English Setter. Her research was accepted by the IKC, and registration of Red and Whites was resumed.

Mrs Cuddy's extensive efforts on behalf of the breed were formally recognised in 1982 when she was invited to judge the breed at Ireland's Swords Championship Show. By now she was arguably the most knowledgeable and experienced Irish Red and White Setter breeder-owner, and the judging assignment honoured her as such.

In April 1977, Mrs Cuddy whelped her last litter of Red and Whites. It produced one perfectly marked Red and White pup, which she sold to Alan and Ann Gormley of Dublin. The Gormleys named him Harlequin of Knockalla, a dog who was to become the trigger for interest in the breed in the United Kingdom.

A Red and White dog (left) and bitch (right). Males are slightly larger and heavier, and tend to carry more coat.

Despite rumours of crosses to this breed, the English Setter, the Irish Red and White's purity was proven, thanks to the tireless efforts of foundation breeder Maureen Cuddy.

Smitten by their new puppy, the Gormleys soon obtained a bitch pup from another prominent breeder of Red and Whites, the Reverend Patrick Doherty. The pup was named Heidi of Meudon, and she was bred twice to Harlequin. Most of the Gormleys' puppies were imported to Great Britain and went on to become very influential in the breed. Meudon pups were later exported also to the United States, Italy and Holland.

Harlequin, however, was still the light of Alan Gormley's life, and together they followed the show circuit all over Ireland, showing under the Gormleys' kennel prefix, Meudon. Although not active in field work, Harlequin ran his qualifying test while still a youngster and completed all the

## TASKS OF THE WORKING SETTER

The advent of the shotgun forever changed the role of the sporting dog and the work that he was bred to do. With birds of prey and netting practices no longer necessary, the dog took on a more active and prominent role as an important partner in the hunting party. His working habits changed, as hunting behind the gun now required that the dog be steady to wing and shot, another conditioned behaviour that continues to be essential in the working setter.

tasks set out by the assessors. Unfortunately, his paperwork became lost and his results were not recorded, robbing him of the opportunity to perhaps become the first Irish champion in the breed.

In 1980, Alan entered Harlequin in the prestigious Crufts in England. Due to another mix-up in paperwork, he was accidentally classified as a red Setter and benched with the all-red Irish Setters. Harlequin created quite a stir at the show due to his unique coat and colour,

The Red and White is a sporting dog and companion dog who owes the current resurgence of interest to the dedicated fanciers who promoted the breed in the 1970s and '80s.

providing evidence 'in the flesh' that the Red and White was not extinct. His appearance sparked great interest and, as a result, several dogs were imported to Britain.

Another breeder of great significance in the resurgence of

**EARLY REFERENCES**
Noted author Gilbert Leighton-Boyce, in his 1985 book *A Survey of Early Setters*, supports Dr Caius' observations and recounts references to 'Spaniels...mostly white with red patches' during the 14th century.

the breed was Dermott Mooney, who bred Red and Whites under his Winnowing prefix. A sportsman who grew up with shooting dogs, Mooney obtained his first Red and White in 1966, a bitch named Charlaville Beauty, who was a good representative of the breed. Beauty was bred twice, to solid working red dogs, producing, unfortunately, mostly mismarked puppies. Mooney built his Winnowing line by keeping only the properly marked bitch pups to breed, breeding them to proven dogs, and producing some excellent field-trial dogs. Some of his more successful breedings were to Alan Gormley's bitches, with several of those pups exported to Britain.

Just as Mrs Cuddy had secured the breed's future in Ireland, the litter of most importance to the revival of the breed in Great Britain was also from Mrs Cuddy's stock. Her Genevieve of Knockalla went to Mrs Audrey Kaulbeck of Bantry Bay, a long-time breeder of Dachshunds who bred her dogs under the Ardnagashel prefix. Totally enamoured with the Red and White, Mrs Kaulbeck mated Genevieve to Mrs Cuddy's George of Knockalla in 1978. The pair produced 12 puppies, all red and white. The pups were listed in an English publication, and three of the bitch pups were imported to England, where they were bred, providing the foundation stock found in many of today's important pedigrees. Although Mrs Kaulbeck later bred several litters and kept certain dogs for herself, that first litter had the most impact on the resurgence of the breed in England.

By 1980, the growing popularity of the Red and White in Britain led naturally to talk of forming a club to continue the revival of the breed. The first formal meeting of enthusiasts took place on 1 March 1981. Three years of paperwork and meetings followed, with the inaugural meeting of the Irish Red and White Setter Club of Great Britain held on 18 March 1983. The club annually hosts a Championship Show, two Open Shows, the IR&W Challenge, breed seminars, Working Days and seminars, eye testing facilities and training for judges. They also publish a yearbook, a code of ethics and updates for member education.

The Irish Red and White Setter is slowly making his mark throughout the world and is gradually being accepted by kennel clubs in various countries; Germany, the United States, Australia, Finland, Sweden and Belgium all have welcomed the Red and White into their show-dog societies. The Fédération Cynologique Internationale (FCI) recognised the breed in 1989.

## ROSSMORE SETTER
The Irish Red and White Setter is often referred to as the Rossmore Setter. The name reflects the efforts of the nobleman, Lord Rossmore, Rossmore Castle of County Monaghan, who maintained an excellent strain of Red and Whites that dated back to the 18th century.

# Characteristics of the
# IRISH RED AND WHITE SETTER

There is no question that the Irish Red and White Setter is an eye-catching animal. Although the breed is known more for its unique long and silky coat, burnished with chestnut red patches, its temperament is equally desirable. This is a friendly and loving dog that is good with children and makes an ideal family pet. Although they are typically Irish in character, with a mischievous and clownish streak, they have a tendency to be rather aloof when first meeting people, as they are inclined to stand back and 'size you up' before offering a friendly paw. They are considered 'late bloomers,' being a bit slower to mature than most other breeds.

The Irish Red and White Setter is smart and sensitive, requiring the more moderate training approach associated with most setter breeds, as he will not tolerate heavy-handed treatment or training methods. However, once he knows he has mastered a task or done something right, he just might drive you crazy in his unrelenting desire to repeat his successful performance! And although he is an highly intelligent animal, he still needs consistent

training tempered with a large dash of patience; a bit of an Irish sense of humour also helps!

Some who have trained both the red Irish Setter and the Irish Red and White Setter claim that the Red and White is easier to train, as it is possessed of a more mellow disposition and is more eager to please. Training is best done in smaller increments at frequent intervals; five or ten minutes once or twice daily will produce far greater results than long sessions of an hour or more at one time. Puppy and next-level obedience classes are strongly recommended to help socialise the young dog and teach him the rudiments of the learning process.

The Irish Red and White Setter needs the same high level of exercise as all the setter breeds...these dogs were bred to run! They do not thrive in small, confined environments where they cannot go off for a good run every day. The adult Red and White will easily outlast his owner on long walks; five or six kilometres daily are the bare minimum to maintain a dog that is healthy in body and in spirit. An under-exercised Red and White will become bored and mischievous, which can lead to an unruly dog that will create chaos, hardly an ideal scenario for either dog or owner. Owners should discourage heavy jumping activities during the dog's first year to prevent stress on the young dog's growing joints.

Although the Red and White is bred to be primarily an hunting dog, a Red and White does not have to be reared in a total hunting environment. In Ireland, the breed has a reputation as an excellent all-purpose gundog with natural retrieving ability. In Great Britain, however, where the breed is more populous, the Red and White is seen more frequently on the bench than in the field, which is no doubt attributable to the dog's remarkable beauty and regal carriage. However, many show

exhibitors, in Great Britain as well as in other countries, still work their dogs in the field, and the breed clubs are making great strides in introducing their members to the working nature of the breed. Red and Whites are natural hunting dogs and will enjoy field work on any level. Their enthusiasm also lends itself well to agility sports.

Irish Red and White Setters require the basic grooming elements of daily maintenance with a comb and brush to keep the coat in good condition. The long feathering on the legs and hindquarters tends to become matted, especially if the dog runs in tall grass or heavy cover. This can be trimmed or thinned to minimise such tangling. The hair

**Show exhibitors in the UK still work their dogs in the field, though the breed is more frequently seen at dog shows than in the hunt.**

## THE SPORTSMAN'S CHOICE

Many sportsmen consider the Red and White superior to the red Irish Setter because of its calmer temperament and because it can be seen more easily in the autumn countryside.

on the long ears can also be trimmed for neatness. Hair between the pads of the feet should be trimmed regularly to prevent mud, snow and ice from accumulating between the toes. Although the Red and White is a naturally clean animal, regular bathing may be necessary to keep the white coat from becoming grey and dingy.

## HEALTH ISSUES

*Special thanks to Ann Millington [Genetic Sub-Committee, Irish Red and White Setter Club of Great Britain (IRWSCGB)] for her contribution to this section.*

Since the Irish Red and White Setter was revived from an handful of dogs in the late 1970s, our breed club, the IRWSCGB, has monitored the health of the breed very carefully. We have a database of all of the Irish Red and Whites born in the UK and some of those born overseas. It is surprising that there are no big health problems. There are common canine conditions reported (some of which are explained further here), but none in enough numbers to be able to see a trend...believe me, if there were, we would be investigating further!

The three diseases for which we have tests were acted upon because there was an hereditary connection and, as we send out regular health questionnaires to our members, we feel that we have our fingers on the pulse of

**CORRECTIVE SURGERY**
Surgery is often used to correct genetic bone diseases in dogs. Usually the problems present themselves early in the dog's life and must be treated before bone growth stops.

the breed—something not easily done in breeds with huge numbers of dogs.

### POSTERIOR POLAR CATARACT (PPC)

Posterior polar cataract is a localised cataract, affecting the back of the eye. There is currently an eye examination programme for PPC, and the IRWSCGB is working towards a DNA test that will enable us to eliminate this condition from the breed.

### CANINE LEUKOCYTE ADHESION DEFICIENCY (CLAD)

This is an inherited immune disorder that affects a dog's ability to combat bacterial infection and is thought to be specific to the Irish Red and White Setter and the Irish Setter, in which it is also called canine granulocytopathy (CGS). The IRWSCGB has a policy that will eradicate this inherited disease in one generation.

CLAD is a defect caused by an absence of leukocyte integrins; leukocytes are white blood cells necessary to protect the body from microorganisms that cause disease and integrins are a group of

receptors that promote cell adhesion. Affected puppies are unable to ward off infections from superficial wounds or lesions and are extremely vulnerable to respiratory infections and complications, as well as highly susceptible to bacterial and fungal infections. They also may have stunted body growth and be in poor physical shape.

CLAD occurs in the first few months of life. At about 10 to 14 weeks of age, pups may develop gingivitis (inflammation of the gums) or inflammation of the joints, especially at the jaws or knees. They will run elevated temperatures and be unable to eat or stand up. Antibiotics provide only a temporary respite, as puppies will relapse as soon as medication is discontinued. The prognosis is very poor for affected animals, and most are humanely euthanised.

Fortunately, a test has been developed to diagnose this disorder, and DNA tests are available to identify carriers. This is an inherited disease, autosomal recessive, meaning that a pup must receive the recessive gene for CLAD in a double dose, one from each of its parents, in order to be affected. Dogs can also be carriers, meaning that they possess the gene for CLAD in a single dose. Carriers do not become affected by the condition;

## DOGS, DOGS, GOOD FOR YOUR HEART!

People usually purchase dogs for companionship, but studies show that dogs can help to improve their owners' health and level of activity, as well as lower a human's risk of coronary heart disease. Without even realising it, when a person puts time into exercising, grooming and feeding a dog, he also puts more time into his own personal health care. Dog owners establish more routine schedules for their dogs to follow, which can have positive effects on a human's health. Dogs also teach us patience, offer unconditional love and provide the joy of having a furry friend to pet!

they will, however, pass the gene to their progeny and thus should never be bred from.

### HIP DYSPLASIA (HD)

Hip dysplasia simply means poor or abnormal development of the hip joint where the ball and socket do not function properly. It is common in most large breeds of dogs and is considered to be an inherited disorder. To diagnose HD, your veterinary surgeon will x-ray your dog and submit those films to the British Veterinary Association and The Kennel Club for evaluation. A severe case of HD can render a working dog worthless in the field or other activities, and even a mild case can cause painful arthritis in the average house dog.

While hip dysplasia is a largely inherited condition, research shows that environmental factors play a significant role in its development. Overfeeding and feeding a diet high in calories (primarily fat) during a large-breed puppy's rapid-growth stages are suspected to be contributing factors in the development of HD. Heavy-bodied and overweight puppies are more at risk than pups with very lean conformation.

The British Veterinary Association has joined with The Kennel Club to help curb the incidence of hip dysplasia in all breeds of dog. Dogs over one year

# DO YOU KNOW ABOUT HIP DYSPLASIA?

Hip dysplasia is a fairly common condition found in pure-bred dogs. When a dog has hip dysplasia, its hind leg has an incorrectly formed hip joint. By constant use of the hip joint, it becomes more and more loose, wears abnormally and may become arthritic.

Hip dysplasia can only be confirmed with an x-ray, but certain symptoms may indicate a problem. Your dog may have a hip dysplasia problem if it walks in a peculiar manner, hops instead of smoothly runs, uses its hind legs in unison (to keep the pressure off the weak joint), has trouble getting up from a prone position or always sits with both legs together on one side of its body. As the dog matures, it may adapt well to life with a bad hip, but in a few years the arthritis develops and many dogs with hip dysplasia become cripples.

Hip dysplasia is considered an inherited disease and only can be diagnosed definitively when the dog is two years old. Some experts claim that a special diet might help your puppy outgrow the bad hip, but the usual treatments are surgical. The removal of the pectineus muscle, the removal of the round part of the femur, reconstructing the pelvis and replacing the hip with an artificial one are all surgical interventions that are expensive, but they are usually very successful. Follow the advice of your veterinary surgeon.

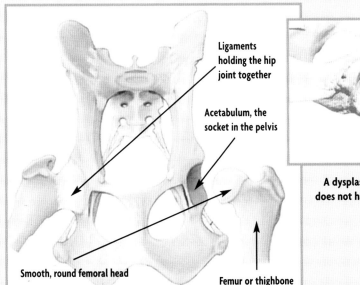

Ligaments holding the hip joint together

Acetabulum, the socket in the pelvis

Smooth, round femoral head

Femur or thighbone

A dysplastic hip. Look at the femoral head; it does not have the smooth surface of the normal one shown at left.

**Normal pelvis with a normal femur or thighbone.**

## DO YOU WANT TO LIVE LONGER?

If you like to volunteer, it is wonderful if you can take your dog to a nursing home once a week for several hours. The elder community loves to have a dog with which to visit, and often your dog will bring a bit of companionship to someone who is lonely or somewhat detached from the world. You will be not only bringing happiness to someone else but also keeping your dog busy—and we haven't even mentioned the fact that it has been discovered that volunteering helps to increase your own longevity!

of age and under six years of age should be x-rayed by a veterinary surgeon. The x-rays are submitted to a special board of veterinary surgeons who specialise in reading orthopaedic films. If the dog shows no evidence of abnormality, a certificate of clearance is issued by The Kennel Club. To correctly identify the dog under evaluation, The Kennel Club requires the dog's date of birth and Kennel Club registration number to be recorded on the x-ray. The purpose of such screening is to eliminate affected dogs from breeding programmes, with the long-term goal of reducing the incidence of HD in the affected breeds.

Irish Red and White Setters who show marked evidence of hip dysplasia should never be bred. Anyone looking for an healthy Red and White pup should make certain the sire and dam of any litter under consideration have their certificates of clearance.

### BLOAT (GASTRIC DILATATION/ VOLVULUS)

Bloat is a life-threatening condition which most commonly occurs in very deep-chested breeds such as the Irish Red and White Setter, Irish Setter, Blood-hound, Great Dane and several other similarly constructed breeds. It occurs when the stomach fills up rapidly with air and begins to twist, cutting off the blood supply.

If not treated immediately, the dog will go into shock and die.

The development of bloat is sudden and unexplainable. The dog will become restless and his stomach will appear swollen or distended, and he will have difficulty breathing. The dog must receive veterinary attention at once in order to survive. The vet must relieve the pressure in the stomach and surgically return the stomach to its normal position.

The IRWSCGB has identified only 6 cases of bloat in the Red and White in the past 20 years, the causes of which were mostly predictable. Nonetheless, research has confirmed that the structure of the setter breeds contributes to their predisposition to this condition and it is worth taking whatever precautions you can take to reduce the risk:

• Feed your dog twice daily rather than offering one large meal.

• Do not exercise your dog for at least an hour before and two hours after he has eaten.

• Make sure your dog is calm and not overly excited while he's eating. It has been shown that nervous or overly excited dogs are more prone to develop bloat.

• Add a small portion of moist meat product to his dried food ration.

• Elevate your dog's bowls in bowl stand, thus avoiding his introducing air into the body by craning his neck when he eats.

### EPILEPSY

Epilepsy is a seizure disorder caused by abnormal electrical patterns in the brain. It affects almost all breeds and even mixed breeds, although some breeds appear to have inherited a predisposition to this disorder.

Primary epilepsy, also known as idiopathic, genetic, inherited or true epilepsy, is difficult to diagnose, and there is no specific test for the disease. Diagnosis is generally drawn by ruling out other possibilities. Primary epilepsy usually occurs between the ages of six months and five years of age.

Secondary epilepsy refers to seizures caused by viral or infectious disease, metabolic disorders, chemical or nutritional imbalance or traumatic injury. Seizures are also associated with hypothyroidism, which is an inherited autoimmune disease common to many pure-bred dogs.

# IRISH RED AND WHITE SETTER

The standards recognised by the Irish Kennel Club and the Kennel Club of Great Britain are quite similar to the one set up by the Irish Red and White Setter Society in 1944. In an important distinction from the bench-bred red Irish Setters, the standard describes the dog as 'athletic rather than racy.' The standard still mandates that the breed be judged as working dogs, possessing those traits most prized by upland gunners, working qualities that have been as carefully preserved as the breed's distinctive colour.

The Irish Red and White Setter's most distinguishing feature is, of course, its coat, with its trademark colour and markings. The predominant colour must be pure white, with 'clear islands' of red markings or patches that are well defined and do not blend at all into the white background. Ticking or flecking is permitted only on the face and legs, but not on the body, which distinguishes the breed from the English Setters with their belton markings.

The head of the Irish Red and White Setter is shorter and broader than that of the red Irish Setter, and lacking the pronounced occipital 'bump' on the skull. The overall impression is one of a robust animal, well-suited to a strenuous day in the field.

Some slight differences exist between the Irish and English Kennel Club standards. The Irish standard is shown in italics within the English standard where differences occur.

**THE KENNEL CLUB STANDARD FOR THE IRISH RED AND WHITE SETTER**

**General Appearance:** Strong and powerful, without lumber—athletic rather than racy.

**Characteristics:** Biddable, highly intelligent, good worker.
*Aristocratic, keen and intelligent.*

**Temperament:** Happy, good natured and affectionate.
*Displays a kindly, friendly attitude behind which should be discernible determination, courage and high spirit.*

**Head and Skull:** Head broad in proportion to the body, with good stop. Skull domed without

In the conforma-
tion ring, the
judge uses the
breed standard to
determine which
dog most closely
conforms to the
ideal description
of the breed.

occiputal protuberance as in Irish Red Setters, fairly square, clean muzzle.

**Eyes:** Hazel or dark brown, slight prominence, and without haw.

**Ears:** Set level with eyes and well back, lying close to the head.

**Mouth:** Jaws strong with a perfect regular scissor bite, i.e. upper teeth closely overlapping lower teeth and set square to the jaws. *Jaws of equal or nearly equal length, regular teeth; scissors bite ideal, level bite acceptable.*

**Neck:** Moderately long, very muscular, but not too thick, slightly arched, free from throatiness.

Comparing the Irish Setter with the Red and White Setter, revealing the Red and White to be more moderate in structure, coat, head type and angulation.

**Forequarters:** Shoulders well laid back. Elbows free, turning neither in nor out. Strong oval bone well muscled, pasterns slightly sloping.

**Body:** Strong and muscular, deep chest and well sprung ribs. Back and quarters very muscular and powerful. Bone strong, well built up with muscle and sinew.

**Hindquarters:** Wide and powerful. Legs from hip to hock long and muscular from hock to heel short and strong. Stifle well bent, hocks well let down turning neither in nor out.

**Feet:** Close-knit, well feathered between toes.

**Gait/Movement:** Long free striding, effortless with drive.
   *When moving at the trot long striding, very lively, graceful and efficient. Head held high, hindquarters drive smoothly and with great power. Forelegs reach* *well ahead and remain low. Seen from front or rear, forelegs and hindlegs below the hock joint moving perpendicularly to the ground; no crossing or weaving of legs, front or back.*

Top: Dog that is coarse and lacking type. The shoulders are loaded, the topline is weak, the toes are out in front and it lacks angulation in the rear. Bottom: Dog that is too extreme, with a domed top skull, straight shoulders, weak pasterns and excessive slope in the topline.

**Tail:** Strong at root, tapering to fine point; with no appearance of ropiness, not reaching below hock. Well feathered, carried level with back or below in lively manner.

**Coat:** Finely textured with good feathering. Slight wave permissible but never curly.
*Long silky fine hair called 'feathering' on the back of the fore and hind legs and on the outer ear flap. Also a reasonable amount on the flank extending on to the chest and throat forming a fringe. All feathering straight, flat and not overly profuse. The tail should be well feathered. On the head, front of legs and other parts of the body, the hair should be short, flat and free from curl, but slight wave is permissible.*

**Colour:** Clearly particoloured, i.e. base colour pearl white, solid red patches. Mottling or flecking but not roaning permitted around the

**THE IDEAL SPECIMEN**
According to The Kennel Club, 'The Breed Standard is the "Blueprint" of the ideal specimen in each breed approved by a governing body, e.g. The Kennel Club, the Fédération Cynologique Internationale (FCI) and the American Kennel Club.
'The Kennel Club writes and revises Breed Standards taking account of the advice of Breed Councils/Clubs. Breed Standards are not changed lightly to avoid "changing the standard to fit the current dogs" and the health and well-being of future dogs is always taken into account when new standards are prepared or existing ones altered.'

face and feet and up foreleg to elbow and up hindleg to hock.
*...roaning, flecking and mottling on any other part of the body is most objectionable and is to be heavily penalised.*

**Size:** Desirable height at withers: dogs 62.2–66 cms (24.5 inches); bitches 57.2–61 cms (22.5–24 inches).

**Faults:** Any departure from the foregoing points should be considered a fault and the seriousness with which the fault should be regarded should be in exact proportion to its degree.

**Note:** Male animals should have two apparently normal testicles fully descended into the scrotum.

The Irish Red and White Setter is clearly a particoloured dog, with some mottling or flecking acceptable on the face, feet and legs.

# IRISH RED AND WHITE SETTER

## WHERE TO BEGIN?

If you are convinced that the Irish Red and White Setter is the ideal dog for you, it's time to learn about where to find a puppy and what to look for. To begin your search for a Red and White puppy, you should enquire about breeders in your area who enjoy a good reputation in the breed. You are looking for an established breeder with outstanding dog ethics and a strong commitment to the breed. New owners should have as many questions as they have doubts. An established breeder is indeed the one to answer your four million questions and make you comfortable with your choice of the Irish Red and White Setter.

An established breeder will sell you a puppy at a fair price if, and only if, the breeder determines that you are a suitable, worthy owner of his dogs. The breeder should make as many enquiries of you as you do of him. Just as you want to choose your breeder with the utmost care, the breeder wants to ensure that his puppies are going to suitable homes

### PREPARING FOR PUP

Unfortunately, when a puppy is bought by someone who does not take into consideration the time and attention that dog ownership requires, it is the puppy who suffers when he is either abandoned or placed in a shelter by a frustrated owner. So all of the 'homework' you do in preparation for your pup's arrival will benefit you both. The more informed you are, the more you will know what to expect and the better equipped you will be to handle the ups and downs of raising a puppy. Hopefully, everyone in the household is willing to do his part in raising and caring for the pup. The anticipation of owning a dog often brings a lot of promises from excited family members: 'I will walk him every day,' 'I will feed him,' 'I will house-train him,' etc., but these things take time and effort, and promises can easily be forgotten once the novelty of the new pet has worn off.

## BOY OR GIRL?

An important consideration to be discussed is the sex of your puppy. In the Irish Red and White, gender differences are slight, and personality is based more on the individual than on its gender. It is always advisable to spay or neuter your pet, which may guarantee your Red and White a longer life.

*The Irish Red and White is an active breed, and the puppies can be rambunctious. Are you ready to invite such chaos into your home?*

and will be well-cared-for. An established breeder can be relied upon for advice, no matter what time of day or night. A reputable breeder will accept a puppy back, without questions, should you decide that this is not the right dog for you.

When choosing a breeder, reputation is much more important than convenience of location. Do not be overly impressed by breeders who run brag advertisements in the dog presses about their stupendous champions. The real quality breeders are quiet and unassuming. You hear about them at the dog shows and field trials, by word of mouth.

## DOCUMENTATION

Two important documents you will get from the breeder are the pup's pedigree and registration certificate. The breeder should register the litter and each pup with The Kennel Club, and it is necessary for you to have the paperwork if you plan on showing or breeding in the future.

Make sure you know the breeder's intentions on which type of registration he will obtain for the pup. There are limited registrations which may prohibit the dog from being shown, bred or competing in non-conformation trials such as Working or Agility if the breeder feels that the pup is not of sufficient quality to do so. There is also a type of registration that will permit the dog in non-conformation competition only.

On the reverse side of the registration certificate, the new owner can find the transfer section, which must be signed by the breeder.

Choosing a breeder is an important first step in dog ownership. Fortunately, the majority of Irish Red and White Setter breeders is devoted to the breed and its well-being. The Kennel Club is able to recommend breeders of quality Irish Red and Whites, as can any local all-breed club or the IRWSCGB.

Potential owners are encouraged to attend dog shows (or trials) to see the Irish Red and White Setters in action, to meet the owners and handlers firsthand and to get an idea of what Red and Whites look like outside a photographer's lens. Provided you approach the handlers when they are not terribly busy with the dogs, most are more than willing to answer questions, recommend breeders and give advice.

Once you have contacted and met a breeder or two and made your choice about which breeder is best suited to your needs, it's time to visit the litter. Keep in mind that many top breeders have waiting lists, or sometimes a litter may not be available immediately. Sometimes new owners have to wait as long as two years for a puppy. If you are really committed to the breeder whom you've selected, then you will wait (and hope for an early arrival!). If not, you may have to continue your search for another breeder with whom you feel comfortable. Don't be too anxious, however. If the breeder doesn't have a waiting list, or any customers, there is probably a good reason. It's no different than visiting a pub with no clientele. The better pubs and restaurants always have waiting lists—and it's usually worth the wait.

### 'YOU BETTER SHOP AROUND!'

Finding a reputable breeder that sells healthy pups is very important, but make sure that the breeder you choose is not only someone you respect but also someone with whom you feel comfortable. Your breeder will be a resource long after you buy your puppy, and you must be able to call with reasonable questions without being made to feel like a pest! If you don't connect on a personal level, investigate some other breeders before making a final decision.

Besides, isn't a puppy more important than a pint?

Since you are likely to be choosing a Red and White as a pet dog and not a show dog, you simply should select a pup that is friendly, attractive and healthy. Irish Red and White Setters have good-sized litters, ranging from six pups to a dozen, with seven or eight being more common, so you will have a considerable selection from which to choose. If you are choosing a pup for eventual showing or field work, this should be made clear to the breeder so that he can help you select the pup that shows the most promise for the ring, the field, etc.

Health in the puppies should be evident: shiny coat, clear eyes, alert disposition, etc; all puppies in the litter should be healthy. Always check the bite of your selected puppy to be sure that it is neither

Irish Red and Whites have large litters, and the selection of a puppy is often overwhelming. Discuss your lifestyle and needs with the breeder, and he will be able to recommend the kind of puppy that should best fit your world.

**ARE YOU A FIT OWNER?**
If the breeder from whom you are buying a puppy asks you a lot of personal questions, do not be insulted. Such a breeder wants to be sure that you will be a fit provider for his puppy.

overshot nor undershot. This may not be too noticeable on a young puppy, but will become more evident as the puppy gets older.

You should consider whether you want a male or female puppy. The differences between the male and female Red and White are not terribly significant; differences are more those of individual personality rather than gender. The obvious physical difference is that the male is taller and heavier. Bitches also have a season every six to nine months, although if you have her spayed after her first season, as you should with a pet, this will not present a problem. The female also is inclined to have less coat than the male, especially in the summer. Some claim the male is more loyal, and the bitch more independent. Again, I believe that such differences are based on the individual dog, not on the gender.

Breeders commonly allow visitors to see their litters by

## HANDLE WITH CARE

You should be extremely careful about handling tiny puppies. Not that you might hurt them, but that the pups' mother may exhibit what is called 'maternal aggression.' It is a natural, instinctive reaction for the dam to protect her young against anything she interprets as predatory or possibly harmful to her pups. The sweetest, most gentle of bitches, after whelping a litter, often reacts this way, even to her owner.

around the fifth or sixth week, and puppies leave for their new homes between the eighth and tenth week. Breeders who permit their puppies to leave early are more interested in your pounds than in their puppies' well-being. Puppies

## INSURANCE

Many good breeders will offer you insurance with your new puppy, which is an excellent idea. The first few weeks of insurance will probably be covered free of charge or with only minimal cost, allowing you to take up the policy when this expires. If you own a pet dog, it is sensible to take out such a policy as veterinary fees can be high, although routine vaccinations and boosters are not covered. Look carefully at the many options open to you before deciding which suits you best.

need to learn the rules of the pack from their dams, and most dams continue teaching the pups manners and dos and don'ts until around the eighth week. Breeders spend significant amounts of time with the Red and White toddlers so that the pups are able to interact with the 'other species,' i.e. humans. Given the long history

that dogs and humans have, bonding between the two species is natural but must be nurtured. A well-bred, well-socialised Irish Red and White Setter pup wants nothing more than to be near you and please you.

## COMMITMENT OF OWNERSHIP

After considering all of these factors, you have most likely already made some very

The rapport between the dam and her pups speaks volumes about the temperament of the litter and the breeder's line. A patient, loving dam yields puppies with these same desirable traits.

## PUPPY APPEARANCE

Your puppy should have a well-fed appearance but not a distended abdomen, which may indicate worms or incorrect feeding, or both. The body should be firm, with a solid feel. The skin of the abdomen should be pale pink and clean, without signs of scratching or rash. Check the hind legs to make certain that dewclaws were removed, if any were present at birth.

important decisions about selecting your puppy. You have chosen an Irish Red and White Setter, which means that you have decided which characteristics you want in a dog and which type of dog will best fit into your family and lifestyle. If you have selected a breeder, you have gone a step further—you have done your research and found a responsible, conscientious person who breeds quality Irish Red and White Setters and who should be a reliable source of help as you and your puppy adjust to life together. If you have observed a litter in action, you have obtained a firsthand look at the dynamics of a puppy 'pack' and, thus, you have learned about each pup's individual personality—perhaps you have even found one that particularly appeals to you.

However, even if you have not yet found the Irish Red and White Setter puppy of your dreams, observing pups will help you learn to recognise certain behaviour and to determine what a pup's behaviour indicates about his temperament. You will be able to pick out which pups are the leaders, which ones are less outgoing, which ones are confident, which ones are shy, playful, friendly, aggressive, etc. Equally as important, you will learn to recognise what an

fun—it should not be so serious and so much work. Keep in mind that your puppy is not a cuddly stuffed toy or decorative lawn ornament; rather, he is a living creature that will become a real member of your family. You will come to realise that, while buying a puppy is a pleasurable and exciting

healthy pup should look and act like. All of these things will help you in your search, and when you find the Irish Red and White Setter that was meant for you, you will know it! Remember, you are choosing a companion that will be with you for upwards of 10 years, so it's worth it to take time with your search.

Researching your breed, selecting a responsible breeder and observing as many pups as possible are all important steps on the way to dog ownership. It may seem like a lot of effort... and you have not even taken the pup home yet! Remember, though, you cannot be too careful when it comes to deciding on the type of dog you want and finding out about your prospective pup's background. Buying a puppy is not—or should not be—just another whimsical purchase. This is one instance in which you actually do get to choose your own family! You may be thinking that buying a puppy should be

**HOW VACCINES WORK**
If you've just bought a puppy, you surely know the importance of having your pup vaccinated, but do you understand how vaccines work? Vaccines contain the same bacteria or viruses that cause the disease you want to prevent, but they have been chemically modified so that they don't cause any harm. Instead, the vaccine causes your dog to produce antibodies that fight the harmful bacteria. Thus, if your dog is exposed to the disease in the future, the antibodies will destroy the viruses or bacteria.

## TIME TO GO HOME

Breeders rarely release puppies until they are eight to ten weeks of age. This is an acceptable age for most breeds of dog, excepting toy breeds, which are not released until around 12 weeks, given their petite sizes. If a breeder has a puppy that is 12 weeks of age or older, it is likely well socialised and house-trained. Be sure that it is otherwise healthy before deciding to take it home.

basic needs for survival. In addition to food, water and shelter, your pup needs care, protection, guidance and love. If you are not prepared to commit to this, then you are not prepared to own a dog.

Wait a minute, you say. How hard could this be? All of my neighbours own dogs and they seem to be doing just fine. Why should I have to worry about all of this? Well, you should not worry about it; in fact, you will probably find that once your Irish Red and White Setter pup gets used to his new home, he will fall into his place in the family quite naturally. However, it never hurts to emphasise the commitment of dog ownership. With some time and patience, it is really not too difficult to raise a curious and exuberant Irish Red and White Setter pup to be a well-adjusted and well-mannered adult dog—a dog that could be your most loyal friend.

endeavour, it is not something to be taken lightly. Relax...the fun will start when the pup comes home!

Always keep in mind that a puppy is nothing more than a baby in a furry disguise...a baby who is virtually helpless in a human world and who trusts his owner for fulfilment of his

## INHERIT THE MIND

In order to know whether or not a puppy will fit into your lifestyle, you need to assess his personality. A good way to do this is to interact with his parents. Your pup inherits not only his appearance but also his personality and temperament from the sire and dam. If the parents are fearful or overly aggressive, these same traits may likely show up in your puppy.

## PUPPY SELECTION

Your selection of a good puppy can be determined by your needs. A show potential or a good pet? It is your choice. Every puppy, however, should be of good temperament. Although show-quality puppies are bred and raised with emphasis on physical conformation, responsible breeders strive for equally good temperament. Do not buy from a breeder who concentrates solely on physical beauty at the expense of personality.

## PREPARING PUPPY'S PLACE IN YOUR HOME

Researching your breed and finding a breeder are only two aspects of the 'homework' you will have to do before taking your Irish Red and White Setter puppy home. You will also have to prepare your home and family for the new addition. Much as you would prepare a nursery for a newborn baby, you will need to designate a place in your home that will be the puppy's own. How you prepare your home will depend on how much freedom the dog will be allowed. Whatever you decide, you must ensure that he has a place that he can 'call his own.'

When you bring your new puppy into your home, you are bringing him into what will become his home as well. Obviously, you did not buy a puppy with the intentions of catering to his every whim and allowing him to 'rule the roost,' but in order for a puppy to grow into a stable, well-adjusted dog, he has to feel comfortable in his surroundings. Remember, he is leaving the warmth and security of his mother and littermates, as well as the familiarity of the only place he has ever known, so it is important to make his transition as easy as possible. By preparing a place in your home for the puppy, you are making him feel as welcome as possible in a strange new place. It should not take him long to get used to it, but the sudden shock of being transplanted is somewhat traumatic for a young pup. Imagine how a small child would feel in the same

If you are seeking to adopt a puppy for showing, discuss this with your chosen breeder. You may have to wait longer for a show-quality puppy, which will likely be more expensive than a pet-quality dog.

Your local pet shop should have crates large enough for the fully-grown Red and White.

not the case at all. Although all breeders do not advocate crate training, more and more breeders and trainers are recommending crates as preferred tools for show puppies as well as pet puppies.

Crates are not cruel—crates have many humane and highly effective uses in dog care and training. For example, crate training is a very popular and

## PUPPY PERSONALITY

When a litter becomes available to you, choosing a pup out of all those adorable faces will not be an easy task! Sound temperament is of utmost importance, but each pup has its own personality and some may be better suited to you than others. A feisty, independent pup will do well in an home with older children and adults, while quiet, shy puppies will thrive in an home with minimal noise and distractions. Your breeder knows the pups best and should be able to guide you in the right direction.

situation—that is how your puppy must be feeling. It is up to you to reassure him and to let him know, 'Little chap, you are going to like it here!'

## WHAT YOU SHOULD BUY

### CRATE

To someone unfamiliar with the use of crates in dog training, it may seem like punishment to shut a dog in a crate, but this is

**CRATE TRAINING TIPS**
During crate training, you should partition off the section of the crate in which the pup stays. If he is given too big an area, this will hinder your training efforts. Crate training is based on the fact that a dog does not like to soil his sleeping quarters, so it is ineffective to keep a pup in a crate that is so big that he can eliminate in one end and get far enough away from it to sleep. Also, you want to make the crate den-like for the pup. Blankets and a favourite toy will make the crate cosy for the small pup; as he grows, you may want to evict some of his 'roommates' to make more room.

It will take some coaxing at first, but be patient. Given some time to get used to it, your pup will adapt to his new home-within-an-home quite nicely.

very successful house-training method. In addition, a crate can keep your dog safe during travel and, perhaps most importantly, a crate provides your dog with a place of his own in your home. It serves as a 'doggie bedroom' of sorts—your Irish Red and White Setter can curl up in his crate when he wants to sleep or when he just needs a break. Many dogs sleep in their crates overnight. With soft bedding and his favourite toy, a crate becomes a cosy pseudo-den for your dog. Like his ancestors, he too will seek out the comfort and retreat of a den—you just happen to be providing him with something a little more luxurious than what his early ancestors enjoyed.

As far as purchasing a crate, the type that you buy is up to you. It will most likely be one of the two most popular types: wire or fibreglass. There are advantages and disadvantages to each type. For example, a wire crate is more open, allowing the air to flow through and affording the dog a view of what is going on around him, while a fibreglass crate is sturdier. Both

Breeders commonly introduce puppies to crates as part of their early training and socialisation. These two pups are exploring a medium-size wire crate.

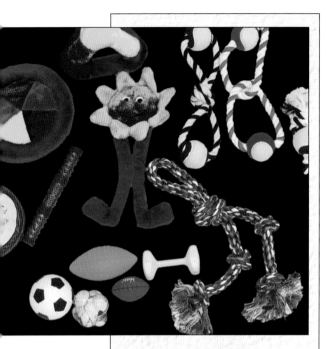

### TOYS, TOYS, TOYS!

With a big variety of dog toys available, and so many that look like they would be a lot of fun for a dog, be careful in your selection. It is amazing what a set of puppy teeth can do to an innocent-looking toy, so, obviously, safety is a major consideration. Be sure to choose the most durable products that you can find. Hard nylon bones and toys are a safe bet, and many of them are offered in different scents and flavours that will be sure to capture your dog's attention. It is always fun to play a game of catch with your dog, and there are balls and flying discs that are specially made to withstand dog teeth.

can double as travel crates, providing protection for the dog. The size of the crate is another thing to consider. Puppies do not stay puppies forever—in fact, sometimes it seems as if they grow right before your eyes. A small crate may be fine for a very young Irish Red and White Setter pup, but it will not do him much good for long! Unless you have the money and the inclination to buy a new crate every time your pup has a growth spurt, it is better to get one that will accommodate your dog both as a pup and at full size. A suitable crate for the Red and White should be at least 56 cms (22 inches) wide by 91.5 cms (36 inches) long, and high enough so that the dog can stand comfortably.

BEDDING

Veterinary bedding in the dog's crate will help the dog feel more at home, and you may also like to pop in a small blanket. First, this will take the place of the leaves, twigs, etc., that the pup would use in the wild to make a den; the pup can make his own 'burrow' in the crate. Although your pup is far removed from his den-making ancestors, the denning instinct is still a part of his genetic makeup. Second, until you take your pup home, he has been sleeping amid the warmth of his mother and littermates, and while a blanket is not the same as a warm, breathing body, it still provides heat and something with which to snuggle. You will want to wash your pup's bedding frequently in case he has a toileting 'accident' in his crate, and replace or remove any blanket that becomes ragged and starts to fall apart.

## Toys

Toys are a must for dogs of all ages, especially for curious playful pups. Puppies are the 'children' of the dog world, and what child does not love toys? Chew toys provide enjoyment for both dog and owner—your dog will enjoy playing with his favourite toys, while you will enjoy the fact that they distract him from chewing on your expensive shoes and leather sofa. Puppies love to chew; in fact, chewing is a physical need for pups as they are teething,

and everything looks appetising! The full range of your possessions—from old tea towel to Oriental carpet—are fair game

### YOUR SCHEDULE...

If you lead an erratic, unpredictable life, with daily or weekly changes in your work requirements, consider the problems of owning a dog. The new puppy has to be fed regularly, socialised (loved, petted, handled, introduced to other people) and, most importantly, allowed to visit outdoors for toilet training. As the dog gets older, it can be more tolerant of deviations in its feeding and toilet relief.

### MENTAL AND DENTAL

Toys not only help your puppy get the physical and mental stimulation he needs but also provide a great way to keep his teeth clean. Hard rubber or nylon toys, especially those constructed with grooves, are designed to scrape away plaque, preventing bad breath and gum infection.

in the eyes of a teething pup. Puppies are not all that discerning when it comes to finding something literally to 'sink their teeth into'— everything tastes great! The Red and White is a natural retriever, which means that they tend to be more oral than most breeds.

Only hard, durable toys should be offered to the Irish Red and White. Hard sterile bones, nylon bones and other indestructible chew devices are good choices. Breeders advise owners to resist stuffed toys, because they can become de-stuffed in no time. The overly excited pup may ingest the stuffing, which is neither nutritious nor digestible.

Similarly, squeaky toys are quite popular, but must be avoided for the Irish Red and White Setter. Perhaps a squeaky toy can be used as an aid in training, but not for free play. If a pup 'disembowels' one of these, the small plastic squeaker inside can be dangerous if swallowed. Monitor the condition of all your pup's toys carefully and get rid of any that have been chewed to the point of becoming potentially dangerous.

Be careful of natural bones, which have a tendency to splinter into sharp, dangerous pieces. Also be careful of rawhide, which can turn into pieces that are easy to swallow and become a mushy mess on your carpet.

## LEAD

A nylon lead is probably the best option, as it is the most resistant to puppy teeth should your pup take a liking to chewing on his lead. Of course, this is an habit that should be nipped in the bud, but, if your pup likes to chew on his lead, he has a very slim chance of being able to chew through the strong nylon. Nylon leads are also lightweight, which is good for a young Irish Red and White Setter who is just getting used to the idea of walking on a lead.

For everyday walking and safety purposes, the nylon lead

# CHOOSE AN APPROPRIATE COLLAR

The **BUCKLE COLLAR** is the standard collar used for everyday purposes. Be sure that you adjust the buckle on growing puppies. Check it every day. It can become too tight overnight! These collars can be made of leather or nylon. Attach your dog's identification tags to this collar.

The **CHOKE COLLAR** is constructed of highly polished steel so that it slides easily through the stainless steel loop. The idea is that the dog controls the pressure around its neck and he will stop pulling if the collar becomes uncomfortable. It should *not* be used with the Red and White.

The **HALTER** is for a trained dog that has to be restrained to prevent running away, chasing a cat and the like. Considered the most humane of all collars, it is frequently used on smaller dogs for which collars are not comfortable.

Purchase the best-quality bowls that your pet shop has to offer. Bowl stands should also be available, which are useful for preventing bloat in deep-chested breeds like the Irish Red and White.

is a good choice. As your pup grows up and gets used to walking on the lead, you may want to purchase a flexible lead. These leads allow you to extend the length to give the dog a broader area to explore or to shorten the length to keep the dog near you. Of course, there are leads designed for training purposes and specially made leather harnesses, but these are not necessary for routine walks.

## COLLAR

Your pup should get used to wearing a collar all the time since you will want to attach his ID tags to it; plus, you have to attach the lead to something! A lightweight nylon collar is a good choice. Make certain that the collar fits snugly enough so that the pup cannot wriggle out of it, but is loose enough so that it will not be uncomfortably tight around the pup's neck. You should be able to fit a finger between the pup's neck and the collar. It may take some time for your pup to get used to wearing the collar, but soon he will not even notice that it is there. Choke collars are made for training, but are not recommended for use with the Irish Red and White, a breed that does not respond to harsh training methods and requires positive reinforcement and encouragement in training.

## FOOD AND WATER BOWLS

Your pup will need two bowls, one for food and one for water. You may want two sets of bowls, one for indoors and one for outdoors, depending on where the dog will be fed and where he will be spending time. Stainless steel or sturdy plastic bowls are popular choices. Plastic bowls are more chewable, but dogs tend not to chew on the steel variety, which can be sterilised. It is important to buy sturdy bowls since anything is in danger of being chewed by puppy teeth and you do not want your dog to be constantly chewing apart his bowl (for his safety and for your purse!).

Bowl stands on which to elevate the Red and White's food and water bowls are recommended. This eliminates the dog's need to crane his neck to eat and drink, and is a proven way to reduce the risk of bloat.

## CLEANING SUPPLIES

Until a pup is house-trained, you will be doing a lot of cleaning. 'Accidents' will occur, which is acceptable in the beginning stages of toilet training because the puppy does not know any better. All you can do is be prepared to clean up any accidents as soon as they happen. Old rags, towels,

### PLAY'S THE THING

Teaching the puppy to play with his toys in running and fetching games is an ideal way to help the puppy develop muscle, learn motor skills and bond with you, his owner and master.

He also needs to learn how to inhibit his bite reflex and never to use his teeth on people, forbidden objects and other animals in play. Whenever you play with your puppy, you make the rules. This becomes an important message to your puppy in teaching him that you are the pack leader and control everything he does in life. Once your dog accepts you as his leader, your relationship with him will be cemented for life.

depending on your situation, but it is important that you have everything you need to feed and make your Irish Red and White Setter comfortable in his first few days at home.

### PUPPY-PROOFING YOUR HOME

Aside from making sure that your Irish Red and White Setter will be comfortable in your home, you also have to make sure that your home is safe for your Irish Red and White Setter. This means taking precautions that your pup will not get into anything he should not get into and that there is nothing within his reach that may harm him should he sniff it, chew it, inspect it, etc. This probably seems obvious since, while you are primarily concerned with your pup's safety, at the same time you do not want your belongings to be ruined. Breakables should be placed out of reach if your dog is to have full run of the house. If he is to

**NATURAL TOXINS**
Examine your grass and garden landscaping before bringing your puppy home. Many varieties of plants have leaves, stems or flowers that are toxic if ingested, and you can depend on a curious puppy to investigate them. Ask your vet for information on poisonous plants or research them at your library.

newspapers and a safe disinfectant are good to have on hand.

BEYOND THE BASICS
The items previously discussed are the bare necessities. You will find out what else you need as you go along—grooming supplies, flea/tick protection, baby gates to partition a room, etc. These things will vary

**CHEMICAL TOXINS**
Scour your garage for potential puppy dangers. Remove weed killers, pesticides and antifreeze materials. Antifreeze is highly toxic and even a few drops can kill a puppy or adult dog. The sweet taste attracts the animal, who will quickly consume it from the floor or curbside.

be limited to certain places within the house, keep any potentially dangerous items in the 'off-limits' areas.

An electrical cord can pose a danger should the puppy decide to taste it—and who is going to convince a pup that it would not make a great chew toy? Cords should be fastened tightly against the wall. If your dog is going to spend time in a crate, make sure that there is nothing near his crate that he can reach if he sticks his curious little nose or paws through the openings. Just as you would with a child, keep all household cleaners and chemicals where the pup cannot reach them.

It is also important to make sure that the outside of your

## TOXIC PLANTS

Many plants can be toxic to dogs. If you see your dog carrying a piece of vegetation in his mouth, approach him in a quiet, disinterested manner, avoid eye contact, pet him and gradually remove the plant from his mouth. Alternatively, offer him a treat and maybe he'll drop the plant on his own accord. Be sure no toxic plants are growing in your own garden.

Expect your inquisitive setter puppy to explore everything in your garden. You should be certain that your Red and White puppy does not have access to any potentially dangerous plants or chemicals, such as antifreeze or rose fertilisers.

**FINANCIAL RESPONSIBILITY**
Grooming tools, collars, leashes, dog beds and, of course, toys will be an expense to you when you first obtain your pup, and the cost will continue throughout your dog's lifetime. If your puppy damages or destroys your possessions (as most puppies surely will!) or something belonging to a neighbour, you can calculate additional expense. There is also flea and pest control, which every dog owner faces more than once. You must be able to handle the financial responsibility of owning a dog.

Always clean up after your dog has relieved itself. Your local pet shop will have aids to make the task easier.

home is safe. Of course, your puppy should never be unsupervised, but a pup let loose in the garden will want to run and explore, and he should be granted that freedom. Do not let a fence give you a false sense of security; you would be surprised at how crafty (and persistent) a dog can be in working out how to dig under and squeeze his way through small holes, or to jump or climb over a fence. While the Irish Red and White Setter is not generally known as a climber, many breeders claim that the Red and White loves to sit up high to view his kingdom, a trait that could lead to 'over the fence' if his house or a table is too close to perimeter of the garden.

The remedy is to make the fence well embedded into the ground and high enough so that it really is impossible for your dog to get over it (between 2-3 metres should suffice). Be sure to repair or secure any gaps in the fence. Check the fence periodically to ensure that it is in good shape and make repairs as needed; a very determined pup may return to the same spot to 'work on it' until he is able to get through.

**FIRST TRIP TO THE VET**
You have selected your puppy, and your home and family are

ready. Now all you have to do is collect your Irish Red and White Setter from the breeder and the fun begins, right? Well…not so fast. Something else you need to plan is your pup's first trip to the veterinary surgeon. Perhaps the breeder can recommend someone in the area who specialises in gundog breeds, or maybe you know some other Irish Red and White Setter owners who can suggest a good vet. Either way, you should have an appointment arranged for your pup before you pick him up.

### SKULL & CROSSBONES

Thoroughly puppy-proof your house before bringing your puppy home. Never use cockroach or rodent poisons or plant fertilisers in any area accessible to the dog. Avoid the use of toilet cleaners. Most dogs are born with 'toilet sonar' and will take a drink if the lid is left open. Also keep the rubbish secured and out of reach.

The pup's first visit will consist of an overall examination to make sure that the pup does not have any problems that are not apparent to you. The veterinary surgeon will also set up a schedule for the pup's vaccinations; the breeder will inform you of which ones the pup has already received and the vet can continue from there.

### FEEDING TIPS

You will probably start feeding your pup the same food that he has been getting from the breeder; the breeder should give you a few days' supply to start you off. Although you should not give your pup too many treats, you will want to have puppy treats on hand for coaxing, training, rewards, etc. Be careful, though, as a small pup's calorie requirements are relatively low and a few treats can add up to almost a full day's worth of calories without the required nutrition.

### INTRODUCTION TO THE FAMILY

Everyone in the family will be excited about the puppy's coming home and will want to pet him and play with him, but it is best to make the introduction low-key so as not to overwhelm the puppy. He is apprehensive already. It is the first time he has been separated from

You should acclimate your new puppy to his crate immediately upon his arrival at your home. The puppy will quickly accept the crate as his home away from home and will soon make himself comfortable there.

his mother and the breeder, and the ride to your home is likely to be the first time he has been in a car. The last thing you want to do is smother him, as this will only frighten him further. This is not to say that human contact is not extremely necessary at this stage, because this is the time when a connection between the pup and his human family is formed. Gentle petting and soothing words should help console him, as well as just putting him down and letting him explore on his own (under your watchful eye, of course).

The pup may approach the family members or may busy himself with exploring for a while. Gradually, each person should spend some time with the pup, one at a time, crouching down to get as close to the pup's level as possible, letting him sniff their hands and petting him gently. He definitely needs human attention and he needs to be touched—this is how to form an immediate bond. Just remember that the pup is experiencing many things for the first time, at the same time. There are new people, new noises, new smells and new things to investigate, so be gentle, be affectionate and be as comforting as you can be.

**PUP'S FIRST NIGHT HOME**
You have travelled home with your new charge safely in his crate. He's been to the vet for a

thorough check-up; he's been weighed, his papers have been examined and perhaps he's even been vaccinated and wormed as well. He's met (and licked!) the whole family, including the excited children and the less-than-happy cat. He's explored his area, his new bed, the garden and anywhere else he's been permitted. He's eaten his first meal at home and relieved himself in the proper place. He's heard lots of new sounds, smelled new friends and seen more of the outside world than ever before...and that was just the first day! He's worn out and is ready for bed...or so you think!

It's puppy's first night home and you are ready to say 'Good night.' Keep in mind that this is his first night ever to be sleeping alone. His dam and littermates are no longer at paw's length and he's a bit scared, cold and lonely. Be reassuring to your new family member, but this is not the time to spoil him and give in to his inevitable whining.

Puppies whine. They whine to let others know where they are and hopefully to get company out of it. Place your pup in his new bed or crate in his designated area and close the door. Mercifully, he may fall asleep without a peep. When the inevitable occurs, however,

ignore the whining—he is fine. Be strong and keep his interest in mind. Do not allow yourself to feel guilty and visit the pup. He will fall asleep eventually.

Many breeders recommend placing a piece of bedding from the pup's former home in his new bed so that he recognises and is comforted by the scent of his littermates. Others still advise placing an hot water bottle in the bed for warmth. The latter may be a good idea provided the pup doesn't

### QUALITY FOOD
The cost of food must be mentioned. All dogs need a good-quality food with an adequate supply of protein to develop their bones and muscles properly. Most dogs are not picky eaters but, unless fed properly, can quickly succumb to skin problems.

**MANNERS MATTER**

During the socialisation process, a puppy should meet people, experience different environments and definitely be exposed to other canines. Through playing and interacting with other dogs, your puppy will learn lessons, ranging from controlling the pressure of his jaws by biting his littermates to the inner-workings of the canine pack that he will apply to his human relationships for the rest of his life. That is why removing a puppy from its litter too early (before eight weeks) can be detrimental to the pup's development.

attempt to suckle—he'll get good and wet, and may not fall asleep so fast.

Puppy's first night can be somewhat stressful for both the pup and his new family. Remember that you are setting the tone of night-time at your house. Unless you want to play with your pup every night at 10 p.m., midnight and 2 a.m., don't initiate the habit. Your family will thank you, and so will your pup!

## PREVENTING PUPPY PROBLEMS

### SOCIALISATION

Now that you have done all of the preparatory work and have helped your pup get accustomed to his new home and family, it is about time for you to have some fun! Socialising your Irish Red and White Setter pup gives you the opportunity to show off your new friend, and your pup gets to reap the benefits of being an adorable furry creature that people will want to pet and, in general, think is absolutely precious!

Besides getting to know his new family, your puppy should be exposed to other people, animals and situations. This will help him become well adjusted as he grows up and less prone to being timid or fearful of the new things he will encounter. Fortunately, the Red and White is not by nature dog-aggressive. Of course, he must not come into close contact with dogs you don't know well until his course of injections is fully complete.

Your pup's socialisation began with the breeder, but now it is your responsibility to continue it. The socialisation he receives until the age of 12 weeks is the most critical, as this is the time when he forms his impressions of the outside world. Be especially careful during the eight-to-ten-week period, also known as the fear period. The interaction he receives during this time should be gentle and reassuring. Lack of socialisation, and/or negative experiences during the sociali-sation period, can manifest itself in fear and aggression as the dog grows up. Your puppy needs lots of positive interac-tion, which of course includes human contact, affection, handling and exposure to other animals.

Once your pup has received his necessary vaccinations, feel free to take him out and about (on his lead, of course). Walk him around the neighbourhood, take him on your daily errands, let people pet him, let him meet other dogs and pets, etc. Puppies do not have to try to make friends; there will be no

## SOCIALISATION

Thorough socialisation includes not only meeting new people but also being introduced to new experiences such as riding in the car, having his coat brushed, hearing the television, walking in a crowd—the list is endless. The more your pup experiences, and the more positive the experiences are, the less of a shock and the less fright-ening it will be for your pup to encounter new things.

**STRESS-FREE**
Some experts in canine health advise that stress during a dog's early years of development can compromise and weaken his immune system, and may trigger the potential for a shortened life expectancy. They emphasise the need for happy and stress-free growing-up years.

too roughly, or an overzealous pup can playfully nip a little too hard. You want to make socialisation experiences positive ones. What a pup learns during this very formative stage will affect his attitude toward future encounters. You want your dog to be comfortable around everyone. A pup that has a bad experience with a child may grow up to be a dog that is shy around or aggressive toward children.

**CONSISTENCY IN TRAINING**
Dogs, being pack animals, naturally need a leader, or else they try to establish dominance in their packs. When you welcome a dog into your family, the choice of who becomes the leader and who becomes the 'pack' is entirely up to you! Your pup's intuitive quest for dominance, coupled with the fact that it is nearly impossible to look at an adorable Irish Red and White Setter pup with his 'puppy-dog' eyes and not cave in, give the pup almost an unfair advantage in getting the upper hand! A pup will definitely test the waters to see what he can and cannot do. Do not give in to those pleading eyes—stand your ground when it comes to disciplining the pup and make sure that all family members do the same. It will only confuse the pup if Mother

shortage of people who will want to introduce themselves. Just make sure that you carefully supervise each meeting. If the neighbourhood children want to say hello, for example, that is great—children and pups most often make great companions. However, sometimes an excited child can unintentionally handle a pup

tells him to get off the sofa when he is used to sitting up there with Father to watch the nightly news. Avoid discrepancies by having all members of the household decide on the rules before the pup even comes home...and be consistent in enforcing them! Early training shapes the dog's personality, so you cannot be unclear in what you expect.

## COMMON PUPPY PROBLEMS

The best way to prevent puppy problems is to be proactive in stopping an undesirable behaviour as soon as it starts. The old saying 'You can't teach an old dog new tricks' does not necessarily hold true, but it is true that it is much easier to discourage bad behaviour in a young developing pup than to wait until the pup's bad behaviour becomes the adult dog's bad habit. There are some problems that are especially prevalent in puppies as they develop.

### NIPPING

As puppies start to teethe, they feel the need to sink their teeth into anything available... unfortunately, that usually includes your fingers, arms, hair and toes. You may find this behaviour cute for the first five seconds...until you feel just how sharp those puppy teeth

are. Nipping is something you want to discourage immediately and consistently with a firm 'No!' (or whatever number of firm 'Nos' it takes for him to understand that you mean business). Then, replace your finger with an appropriate chew toy and praise the pup when he focuses his energy on the toy. While this behaviour is merely

### SOCIALISATION PERIOD

The socialisation period for puppies is from age 8 to 16 weeks. This is the time when puppies need to leave their birth family and take up residence with their new owners, where they will meet many new people, other pets, etc. Failure to be adequately socialised can cause the dog to grow up fearing others and being shy and unfriendly due to a lack of self-confidence.

annoying when the dog is young, it can become dangerous as your Irish Red and White Setter's adult teeth grow in and his jaws develop, and he continues to think it is okay to gnaw on human appendages. Your Red and White does not mean any harm with a friendly nip, but he also does not know his own strength.

## PUPPY PROBLEMS

The majority of problems that are commonly seen in young pups will disappear as your dog gets older. However, how you deal with problems when he is young will determine how he reacts to discipline as an adult dog. It is important to establish who is boss (hopefully it will be you!) straight away when you are first bonding with your dog. This bond will set the tone for the rest of your life together.

## TEETHING TIP

Puppies like soft toys for chewing. Because they are teething, soft items like stuffed toys soothe their aching gums.

### CRYING/WHINING

Your pup will often cry, whine, whimper, howl or make some type of commotion when he is left alone. This is basically his way of calling out for attention to make sure that you know he is there and that you have not forgotten about him. Your puppy feels insecure when he is left alone, when you are out of the house and he is in his crate or when you are in another part of the house and he cannot see you. The noise he is making is an expression of the anxiety he feels at being alone, so he needs to be taught that being alone is okay. You are not actually training the dog to stop making noise; rather, you are training him to feel comfortable when he is alone and thus removing the need for him to make the noise.

This is where the crate with cosy bedding and a toy comes in handy. You want to know that your pup is safe when you are not there to supervise, and you know that he will be safe in his crate rather than roaming freely about the house. In order for the pup to stay in his crate

**TRAINING TIP**

Training your puppy takes much patience and can be frustrating at times, but you should see results from your efforts. If you have a puppy that seems untrainable, take him to a trainer or behaviourist. The dog may have a personality problem that requires the help of a professional, or perhaps you need help in learning how to train your dog.

crate is never used as a form of punishment; this will cause the pup to view the crate as a negative place, rather than as a place of his own for safety and retreat.

Accustom the pup to the crate in short, gradually increasing time intervals in which you put him in the crate, maybe with a treat, and stay in the room with him. If he cries or makes a fuss, do not go to him, but stay in his sight. Gradually he will realise that staying in his crate is all right without your help, and it will not be so traumatic for him when you are not around. You may want to leave the radio on softly when you leave the house; the sound of human voices may be comforting to him.

without making a fuss, he first needs to be comfortable in his crate. On that note, it is extremely important that the

**CHEWING TIPS**

Chewing goes hand in hand with nipping in the sense that a teething puppy is always looking for a way to soothe his aching gums. In this case, instead of chewing on you, he may have taken a liking to your favourite shoe or something else which he should not be chewing. Again, realise that this is a normal canine behaviour that does not need to be discouraged, only redirected. Your pup just needs to be taught what is acceptable to chew on and what is off limits. Consistently tell him NO when you catch him chewing on something forbidden and give him a chew toy. Conversely, praise him when you catch him chewing on something appropriate. In this way you are discouraging the inappropriate behaviour and reinforcing the desired behaviour. The puppy chewing should stop after his adult teeth have come in, but an adult dog continues to chew for various reasons—perhaps because he is bored, needs to relieve tension or just likes to chew. That is why it is important to redirect his chewing when he is still young.

### DIETARY AND FEEDING CONSIDERATIONS

Today the choices of food for your Irish Red and White Setter are many and varied. There are simply dozens of brands of food in all sorts of flavours and textures, ranging from puppy diets to those for seniors. There are even hypoallergenic and low-calorie diets available. Because your Irish Red and White Setter's food has a bearing on coat, health and temperament, it is essential that the most suitable diet is selected for an Irish Red and White Setter of his age. It is fair to say, however, that even experienced owners can be perplexed by the enormous range of foods available. Only understanding what is best for your dog will help you reach an informed decision.

Dog foods are produced in three basic types: dried, semi-moist and tinned. Dried foods are useful for the cost-conscious, for overall they tend to be less expensive than semi-moist or tinned foods. Dried foods also contain the least fat and the most preservatives. In general, tinned foods are made up of 60–70 percent water, while semi-moist ones often contain so much sugar that they are perhaps the least preferred by owners, even though their dogs seem to like them.

**FEEDING TIP**
You must store your dried dog food carefully. Open packages of dog food quickly lose their vitamin value, usually within 90 days of being opened. Mould spores and vermin could also contaminate the food.

When selecting your dog's diet, three stages of development must be considered: the puppy stage, the adult stage and the senior or veteran stage.

## PUPPY STAGE

Puppies instinctively want to suck milk from their mother's teats; a normal puppy will exhibit this behaviour just a few moments following birth. If puppies do not attempt to suckle within the first half-hour or so, they should be encouraged to do so by placing them on the nipples, having selected ones with plenty of milk. This early milk supply is important in providing the essential colostrum, which protects the puppies during the first eight to ten weeks of their lives. Although a mother's milk is much better than any milk formula, despite there being some excellent ones available, if the puppies do not feed, the breeder will have to feed them by hand. For those with less experience, advice from a veterinary surgeon is important so that not only the right quantity of milk is fed but also that of correct quality, fed at suitably frequent intervals, usually every two hours during the first few days of life.

Puppies should be allowed to nurse from their mothers for about the first six weeks,

## FOOD PREFERENCE

Selecting the best dried dog food is difficult. There is no majority consensus among veterinary scientists as to the value of nutrient analyses (protein, fat, fibre, moisture, ash, cholesterol, minerals, etc.). All agree that feeding trials are what matter, but you also have to consider the individual dog. The dog's weight, age and activity level, and what pleases his taste, all must be considered. It is probably best to take the advice of your veterinary surgeon. Every dog's dietary requirements vary, even during the lifetime of a particular dog.

If your dog is fed a good dried food, it does not require supplements of meat or vegetables. Dogs do appreciate a little variety in their diets, so you may choose to stay with the same brand but vary the flavour. Alternatively, you may wish to add a little flavoured stock to give a difference to the taste.

Puppies receive the necessary nourishment and protection from antibodies from their mother's milk. The pups nurse from the dam for the first six to seven weeks.

although, starting around the third or fourth week, the breeder will begin to introduce small portions of suitable solid food. Most breeders like to introduce alternate milk and meat meals initially, building up to weaning time.

By the time the puppies are seven or a maximum of eight weeks old, they should be fully weaned and fed solely on a proprietary puppy food. Selection of the most suitable, good-quality diet at this time is essential, for a puppy's fastest growth rate is during the first year of life. Veterinary surgeons are usually able to offer advice in this regard.

The frequency of meals will be reduced over time, and a young Red and White can be switched to an adult diet around

## CHANGE IN DIET

As your dog's caretaker, you know the importance of keeping his diet consistent, but sometimes when you run out of food or if you're on holiday, you have to make a change quickly. Some dogs will experience digestive problems, but most will not. If you are planning on changing your dog's menu, do so gradually to ensure that your dog will not have any problems. Over a period of four to five days, slowly add some new food to your dog's old food, increasing the percentage of new food each day.

## DO DOGS HAVE TASTE BUDS?

Watching a dog 'wolf' or gobble his food, seemingly without chewing, leads an owner to wonder whether their dogs can taste anything. Yes, dogs have taste buds, with sensory perception of sweet, salty and sour. Puppies are born with fully mature taste buds.

one year of age. Puppy and junior diets should be well balanced for the needs of your dog so that, except in certain circumstances, additional vitamins, minerals and proteins will not be required.

### ADULT DIETS

Although the Irish Red and White reaches full physical maturity around two years of age, the Red and White can be switched to an adult food at the age of about one year. Again you should rely upon your veterinary surgeon or dietary specialist to recommend an acceptable maintenance diet. Major dog-food manufacturers specialise in this type of food, and it is merely necessary for you to select the one best suited to your dog's needs. Active dogs may have different requirements than sedate dogs.

You should purchase bowl stands with which to elevate your Red and White's food and water bowls. This is recommended as a bloat/gastric dilatation preventative measure.

### SENIOR DIETS

As dogs get older, their metabolism changes. The older dog usually exercises less, moves more slowly and sleeps more. This change in lifestyle and physiological performance

## GRAIN-BASED DIETS

Some less expensive dog foods are based on grains and other plant proteins. While these products may appear to be attractively priced, many breeders prefer a diet based on animal proteins and believe that they are more conducive to your dog's health. Many grain-based diets rely on soy protein, which may cause flatulence (passing gas).

There are many cases, however, when your dog might require a special diet. These special requirements should only be recommended by your veterinary surgeon.

# A Worthy Investment

Veterinary studies have proven that a balanced high-quality diet pays off in your dog's overall health, coat quality, behaviour and activity level. Invest in premium brands for the maximum benefit for your dog.

## TEST FOR PROPER DIET

A good test for proper diet is the colour, odour and firmness of your dog's stool. An healthy dog usually produces three semi-hard stools per day. The stools should have no unpleasant odour. They should be the same colour from excretion to excretion.

of age, depending on the dog's activity level and working status, weight, metabolism and overall health. Be sensitive to your senior Irish Red and White

requires a change in diet. Since these changes take place slowly, they might not be recognisable. What is easily recognisable is weight gain. By continuing to feed your dog an adult-maintenance diet when it is slowing down metabolically, your dog will gain weight. Obesity in an older dog compounds the health problems that already accompany old age.

As your dog gets older, few of his organs function up to par. The kidneys slow down and the intestines become less efficient. These age-related factors are best handled with a change in diet and a change in feeding schedule to give smaller portions that are more easily digested. There is no single best diet for every older dog. While many dogs do well on light or senior diets, other dogs do better on puppy diets or other special premium diets such as lamb and rice. The Irish Red and White can be switched to a senior food at about eight years

## FEEDING TIPS

Dog food must be at room temperature, neither too hot nor too cold. Fresh water, changed daily and served in a clean bowl, is mandatory, especially when feeding dried food.

Never feed your dog from the table while you are eating, and never feed your dog leftovers from your own meal. They usually contain too much fat and too much seasoning.

Dogs must chew their food. Hard pellets are excellent; soups and slurries are to be avoided.

Don't add leftovers or any extras to normal dog food. The normal food is usually balanced, and adding something extra destroys the balance.

Except for age-related changes, dogs do not require dietary variations. They can be fed the same diet, day after day, without becoming ill.

To shine as the picture of good health, your Irish Red and White Setter requires proper food, exercise, grooming and companionship.

## TIPPING THE SCALES

Good nutrition is vital to your dog's health, but many people end up over-feeding or giving unnecessary supple-ments. Here are some common doggie diet don'ts:

- Adding milk, yoghurt and cheese to your dog's diet may seem like a good idea for coat and skin care, but dairy products are very fattening and can cause indigestion.
- Diets high in fat will not cause heart attacks in dogs but will certainly cause your dog to gain weight.
- Most importantly, don't assume your dog will simply stop eating once he doesn't need any more food. Given the chance, he will eat you out of house and home!

Setter's diet, as this will help control other problems that may arise with your old friend.

## WATER

Just as your dog needs proper nutrition from his food, water is an essential 'nutrient' as well.

### 'DOES THIS COLLAR MAKE ME LOOK FAT?'

While humans may obsess about how they look and how trim their bodies are, many people believe that extra weight on their dogs is a good thing. The truth is, pets should not be over- or under-weight, as both can lead to or signal sickness. In order to tell how fit your pet is, run your hands over his ribs. Are his ribs buried under a layer of fat or are they sticking out considerably? If your pet is within his normal weight range, you should be able to feel the ribs easily, but they should not protrude abnormally. If you stand above him, the outline of his body should resemble an hourglass. Some breeds do tend to be leaner while some are a bit stockier, but making sure your dog is the right weight for his breed will certainly contribute to his good health.

## THE CANINE GOURMET

Your dog does not prefer a fresh bone. Indeed, he wants it properly aged and, if given such a treat indoors, he is more likely to try to bury it in the carpet than he is to settle in for a good chew! If you have a garden, give him such delicacies outside and guide him to a place suitable for his 'bone yard.' He will carefully place the treasure in its earthy vault and seemingly forget about it. Trust me, his seeming distaste or lack of thanks for your thoughtfulness is not that at all. He will return in a few days to inspect the bone, perhaps to re-bury it, and, when it is just right, he will relish it as much as you do that cooked-to-perfection steak. If he is in a concrete or bricked kennel run, he will be especially frustrated at the hopelessness of the situation. He will vacillate between ignoring it completely, giving it a few licks to speed the curing process with saliva, and trying to hide it behind the water bowl! When the bone has aged a bit, he will set to work on it.

## DRINK, DRANK, DRUNK— MAKE IT A DOUBLE

In both humans and dogs, as well as most other living organisms, water forms the major part of nearly every body tissue. Naturally, we take water for granted, but without it, life as we know it would cease.

For dogs, water is needed to keep their bodies functioning biochemically. Additionally, water is needed to replace the water lost while panting. Unlike humans, who are able to sweat to dissipate heat, dogs must pant to cool down, thereby losing the vital water from their bodies needed to regulate their body temperatures. Humans lose electrolyte-containing products and other body-fluid components through sweating; dogs do not lose anything except water.

Water is essential always, but especially so when the weather is hot or humid or when your dog is exercising or working vigorously.

Water keeps the dog's body properly hydrated and promotes normal function of the body's systems. During house-training, it is necessary to keep an eye on how much water your Irish Red and White Setter is drinking, but once he is reliably trained he should have access to clean fresh water at all times, especially if you feed dried food. Make certain that the dog's water bowl is clean and elevated, and change the water often.

**EXERCISE**

All dogs require some form of exercise, regardless of breed, and the Irish Red and White is quite an active breed. The Red and White needs substantial exercise, consisting of daily runs or brisk walks of two to three miles at least once a day in adulthood. A sedentary lifestyle is as harmful to a dog as it is to a person, and exercising your Irish Red and White Setter can be enjoyable and healthy for both of you.

For the puppy, brisk walks, once the puppy reaches three or four months of age, will stimulate heart rates and build muscle for both dog and owner. Owners should refrain from allowing the Red and White heavy jumping activities during the dog's first year to prevent stress on his growing joints.

Play sessions in the garden and letting the dog run free in the fenced garden under your supervision also are sufficient forms of exercise for the Irish Red and White Setter. Fetching games can be played indoors or out; these are excellent for giving your dog active play that he will enjoy. Chasing things that move comes naturally to dogs of all breeds, and the Red and White is

a natural retriever. When your Irish Red and White Setter runs after the ball or object, praise him for picking it up and encourage him to bring it back to you for another throw. Never go to the object and pick it up yourself, or you'll soon find that you are the one retrieving the objects rather than the dog!

If you choose to play games outdoors, you must have a securely fenced-in garden and/or have the dog attached to at least an 8-metre (25-foot) light line for security. You want your Irish Red and White Setter to run, but not run away!

Bear in mind that an overweight dog should never be suddenly over-exercised; instead he should be encouraged to

increase exercise slowly. Not only is exercise essential to keep the dog's body fit, it is essential to his mental well-being. A bored dog will find something to do, which often manifests itself in some type of destructive behaviour. In this sense, exercise is essential for the owner's mental well-being as well!

## GROOMING

Daily brushing and combing are necessary to keep the Irish Red and White Setter's coat in good condition and free of mats and tangles. The longer feathering requires a bit of extra attention, as it is more susceptible to matting and to attracting dirt and debris from the outdoors. Some owners like to trim or thin the feathering to keep tangling to a minimum. Excess hair between the foot pads should be trimmed, both for neatness and to keep mud, snow and the like from accumulating. The ears can also be tidied up with trimming.

Always check your Irish Red and White's coat for accumulated debris, especially after time spent outdoors. Grooming time is a good time to check the skin and coat for any signs of parasites, irritation or any other abnormalities.

### BATHING
Dogs do not need to be bathed as often as humans, but occasional bathing is essential for healthy skin and an healthy, shiny coat. Irish Red and Whites are naturally clean animals, but bathing will help rid the coat of any dirt picked up outdoors and will keep the white part of the coat looking white! Again, like most anything, if you accustom your pup to being bathed as a puppy, it will be second nature by the time he grows up. You want your dog to be at ease in the bath or else it could end up a wet, soapy, messy ordeal for both of you!

Brush your Irish Red and White Setter thoroughly before wetting his coat. This will get rid of most mats and tangles, which are harder to remove when the coat is wet. Make certain that

Your local pet shop should have the grooming tools you need to keep your Red and White's coat in good condition. You want to buy the best quality tools you can find, so that you don't have to replace them often as your dog grows up.

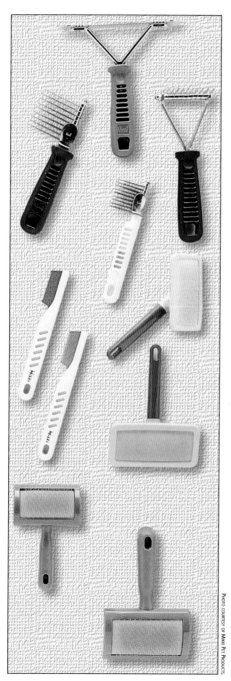

PHOTO COURTESY OF MIKKI PET PRODUCTS.

your dog has a good non-slip surface on which to stand. Begin by wetting the dog's coat, checking the water temperature to make sure that it is neither too hot nor too cold. A shower or hose attachment is necessary for thoroughly wetting and rinsing the coat.

Next, apply shampoo to the dog's coat and work it into a good lather. Wash the head last, as you do not want shampoo to drip into the dog's eyes while you are washing the rest of his body. You should use only a shampoo that is made for dogs. Do not use a product made for human hair. Work the shampoo all the way down to the skin. Do not neglect any area of the body—get all of the hard-to-reach places.

Once the dog has been thoroughly shampooed, he requires an equally thorough rinsing. Shampoo left in the coat can be irritating to the dog's skin. Protect his eyes from the shampoo by shielding them with your hand and directing the flow of water in the opposite direction. You should also avoid getting water in the ear canal. Be prepared for your dog to shake out his coat—you might want to stand back, but make sure you have an hold on the dog to keep him from running through the house.

## EAR CLEANING

The ears should be kept clean with a cotton wipe and ear powder made especially for dogs. The Red and White's ear has small crevices around the ear canal in which wax and debris accumulate. Carefully clean these, but *never* probe into the ear canal, as this can cause injury. Be on the lookout for any signs of infection or ear mite infestation. If your Irish Red and White Setter has been shaking his head or scratching at his ears frequently, this usually indicates a problem. If the dog's ears have an unusual odour, this is a sure sign of mite infestation or infection, and a signal to have his ears checked by the veterinary surgeon.

## NAIL CLIPPING

Your Irish Red and White Setter should be accustomed to having his nails trimmed at an early age since nail clipping will be part of your maintenance routine throughout his life. Not only does it look nicer, but long nails can scratch someone unintentionally. Also, a long nail has a better chance of ripping and bleeding, or causing the feet to spread. A good rule of thumb is that if you can hear your dog's nails' clicking on the floor when he walks, his nails are too long.

Before you start cutting, make sure you can identify the

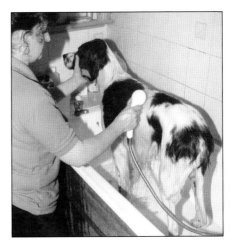

Wet your dog's coat thoroughly before you apply the shampoo.

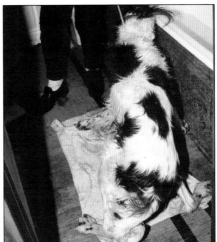

After the bath, you may want to use a lead to restrain your wet setter from running around the house.

Use an heavy towel to dry the dog.

Use a special dog nail clipper to clip the nails. The guillotine-type works the most efficiently on the Red and White.

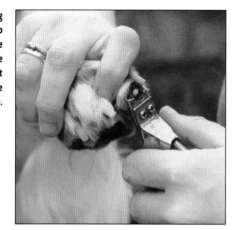

If you cut into the quick and the nail bleeds, apply a clotting agent to the end of the nail to stop the bleeding.

If you've accustomed the young pup to the pedicure procedure, you should have a cooperative adult to work with throughout the dog's life.

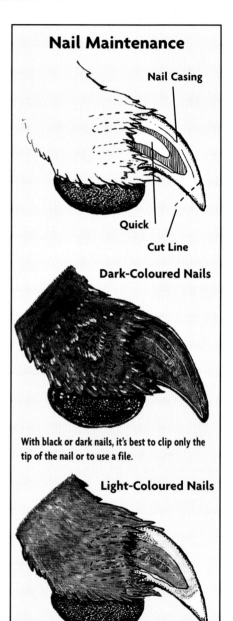

# Nail Maintenance

Nail Casing

Quick

Cut Line

## Dark-Coloured Nails

With black or dark nails, it's best to clip only the tip of the nail or to use a file.

## Light-Coloured Nails

In light-coloured nails, clipping is much simpler because you can see the vein (or quick) that grows inside the casing.

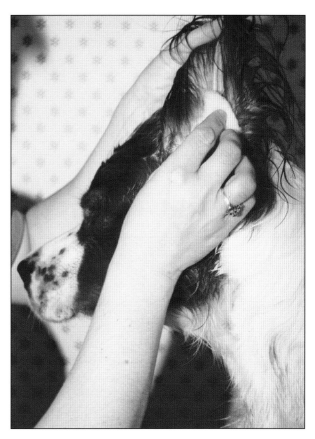

**PEDICURE TIP**

A dog that spends a lot of time outside on an hard surface, such as cement or pavement, will have his nails naturally worn down and may not need to have them trimmed as often, except maybe in the colder months when he is not outside as much. Regardless, it is best to get your dog accustomed to the nail-trimming procedure at an early age so that he is used to it. Some dogs are especially sensitive about having their feet touched, but if a dog has experienced it since puppyhood, it should not bother him.

'quick' in each nail. The quick is a blood vessel that runs through the centre of each nail and grows rather close to the end. The quick will bleed if accidentally cut, which will be quite painful for the dog as it contains nerve endings. Keep some type of clotting agent on hand, such as a styptic pencil or styptic powder (the type used for shaving). This will stop the bleeding quickly when applied to the end of the cut nail. Do not panic if you cut the quick, just stop the bleeding and talk soothingly to your dog. Once he has calmed down, move on to the next nail. It is better to clip a little at a time, particularly with black-nailed dogs.

Hold your pup steady as you begin trimming his nails; you do

Above: Clean the ear with a soft wipe and a specially made ear powder or solution.

Ear cleaning is of utmost importance in this breed. The small indentations around the ear canal need *special* and *careful* attention.

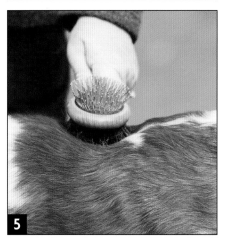

1. Always use a sturdy, non-slip grooming table.

2. Offer a treat for good behaviour.

3. Trim the long hairs of the ears carefully, creating a tidy look.

4. Brush your puppy with a soft brush to acclimate him to the sensation of being groomed.

5. A pin brush and bristle brush are ideal for removing dead coat and tangles from the adult coat.

1. The Irish Red and White sheds hair like any other dog. Grooming reduces the amount of dead hair you'll find floating around your home.

2. Carefully comb the long hairs to rid the feathering of any tangles.

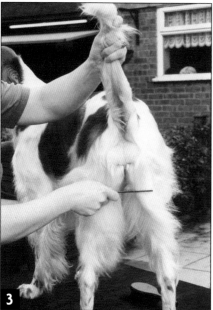

3. Use the comb on the leg furnishings and under the tail, being extra careful in these sensitive areas.

4. Trim the hair between the foot pads. This creates a neat foot while preventing discomfort to the dog.

The teeth and bite of a puppy.

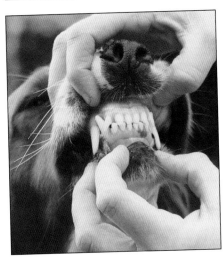

The teeth and bite of an adult.

Scaling the dog's teeth reduces plaque and tartar build-up. Veterinary care is necessary periodically to clean around the gum line.

not want him to make any sudden movements or run away. Talk to him soothingly and stroke him as you clip. Holding his foot in your hand, simply take off the end of each nail with one swift clip. You should purchase nail clippers that are made for use on dogs; you can probably find them wherever you buy grooming supplies.

## TRAVELLING WITH YOUR DOG

### CAR TRAVEL

You should accustom your Irish Red and White Setter to riding in a car at an early age. You may or may not take him in the car often, but at the very least he will need to go to the vet and you do not want these trips to be traumatic for the dog or troublesome for you. The safest way for a dog to ride in the car is in his crate. If he uses a crate in the house, you can use the same crate for travel, provided your vehicle is large enough to accommodate it.

Put the pup in the crate and see how he reacts. If he seems uneasy, you can have a passenger hold him on his lap while you drive. Another option for car travel is a specially made safety harness for dogs, which straps the dog in much like a seat belt. Do not let the dog roam loose in the vehicle—this is very dangerous! If you should stop short, your dog can be thrown and injured. If the dog starts climbing on you and pestering you while you are driving, you will not be able to concentrate on the road. It is an unsafe situation for everyone—human and canine.

For long trips, be prepared to stop to let the dog relieve himself. Take with you whatever you need to clean up after him, including some paper kitchen towels and perhaps some old towelling for use should he have a toileting accident in the car or suffer from travel sickness.

### Air Travel

While it is possible to take a dog on a flight within Britain, this is fairly unusual and advance permission is always required. The dog will be required to travel in a fibreglass crate and you should always check in advance with the airline regarding specific requirements. To help put the dog at ease, give him one of his favourite toys in the crate. Do not feed the dog for several hours before checking in, in order to minimise his need to relieve himself. However, certain regulations specify that water must always be made available to the dog in the crate.

Make sure your dog is properly identified and that your contact information appears on his ID tags and on his crate. Your Red and White will travel in a different area of the plane than human passengers, so every rule must be strictly followed so as to prevent the risk of getting separated from your dog.

### Holidays and Boarding

So you want to take a family holiday—and you want to include *all* members of the family. You would probably make arrangements for accommodation ahead of time anyway, but this is especially important when travelling with a dog. You do not want to make an overnight stop at the only place around for miles, only to find out that they do not allow dogs. Also, you do not want to reserve a place for your family without confirming that you are travelling with a dog, because, if it is against their policy, you may end up without a place to stay.

Alternatively, if you are travelling and choose not to bring your Irish Red and White Setter, you will have to make

**ON THE ROAD**

If you are going on a long motor trip with your dog, be sure the hotels are dog-friendly. Many hotels do not accept dogs. Also take along some ice that can be thawed and offered to your dog if he becomes overheated. Most dogs like to lick ice.

*Select a boarding kennel before you actually need one. Be sure that it is immaculately kept and professionally run. The Red and White will need large runs in order to get proper exercise.*

arrangements for him while you are away. Some options are to take him to a neighbour's house to stay while you are gone, to have a trusted neighbour pop in often or stay at your house or to bring your dog to a reputable boarding kennel. If you choose to board him at a kennel, you should visit in advance to see the facilities provided and where the dogs are kept. Are the dogs' areas spacious and kept clean? Talk to some of the employees and see how they treat the dogs—do they spend time with the dogs, play with them, exercise them, etc.? Also find out

the kennel's policy on vaccinations and what they require. This is for all of the dogs' safety, since there is a greater risk of diseases being passed from dog to dog when dogs are kept together.

### IDENTIFICATION

Your Irish Red and White Setter is your valued companion and friend. That is why you always keep a close eye on him and you have made sure that he cannot

### CONSIDERATIONS ABOUT BOARDING

Will your dog be exercised at least twice a day? How often during the day will the staff keep him company? Does the kennel provide a clean and secure environment? These are some of the questions you should consider when choosing a boarding kennel.

Likewise, if the staff asks you a lot of questions, this is a good sign. They need to know your dog's personality and temperament, health record, special requirements and what commands he has learned. Above all, follow your instincts. If you have a bad feeling about a kennel, even if a friend has recommended it, don't put your dog in their care.

## IDENTIFICATION OPTIONS

As puppies become more and more expensive, especially those puppies of high quality for showing and/or breeding, they have a greater chance of being stolen. The usual collar dog tag is, of course, easily removed. But there are two more permanent techniques that have become widely used for identification.

The puppy microchip implantation involves the injection of a small microchip, about the size of a corn kernel, under the skin of the dog. If your dog shows up at a clinic or shelter, or is offered for resale under less than savoury circumstances, it can be positively identified by the microchip. The microchip is scanned, and a registry quickly identifies you as the owner. This is not only protection against theft, but should the dog run away or go chasing a squirrel and become lost, you have a fair chance of his being returned to you.

Tattooing is done on various parts of the dog, from his belly to his cheeks. The number tattooed can be your telephone number or any other number that you can easily memorise. When professional dog thieves see a tattooed dog, they usually lose interest. Both microchipping and tattooing can be done at your local veterinary clinic. For the safety of our dogs, no laboratory facility or dog broker will accept a tattooed dog as stock.

escape from the garden or wriggle out of his collar and run away from you. However, accidents can happen and there may come a time when your dog unexpectedly becomes separated from you. If this unfortunate event should occur, the first thing on your mind will be finding him. Proper identification, including an ID tag, a tattoo and possibly a microchip, will increase the chances of his being returned to you safely and quickly.

**Trust is the common denominator necessary to teach your dog any command. Once you have secured the Red and White's trust, you will have a loyal, obedient companion for life.**

Living with an untrained dog is a lot like owning a piano that you do not know how to play—it is a nice object to look at, but it does not do much more than that to bring you pleasure. Now try taking piano lessons, and suddenly the piano comes alive and brings forth magical sounds and rhythms that set your heart singing and your body swaying.

The same is true with your Irish Red and White Setter. Any

## THE HAND THAT FEEDS

To a dog's way of thinking, your hands are like his mouth in terms of a defence mechanism. If you squeeze him too tightly, he might just bite you because that would be his normal response. This is not aggressive biting and, although all biting should be discouraged, you need the discipline in learning how to handle your dog.

dog is a big responsibility and, if not trained sensibly, may develop unacceptable behaviour that annoys you or could even cause family friction.

To train your Irish Red and White Setter, you may like to enrol in an obedience class. Teach your dog good manners as you learn how and why he behaves the way he does. Find out how to communicate with your dog and how to recognise and understand his communications with you. Suddenly the dog takes on a new role in your life—he is clever, interesting, well behaved and fun to be with. He demonstrates his bond of devotion to you daily. In other words, your Irish Red and White Setter does wonders for your ego because he constantly reminds you that you are not only his leader, you are his hero!

Those involved with teaching dog obedience and counselling owners about their dogs' behaviour have discovered some interesting facts about dog ownership. For example, training dogs when they are puppies results in the highest rate of success in developing well-mannered and well-adjusted adult dogs. Training an older dog, from six months to six years of age, can produce almost equal results, providing that the owner accepts the dog's slower rate of learning capability and is willing to work patiently to help the dog succeed at developing to his fullest potential. Unfortunately, many owners of untrained adult dogs lack the patience factor, so they do not persist until their dogs are successful at learning particular behaviours.

Training a puppy aged 10 to 16 weeks (20 weeks at the most) is like working with a dry sponge in a pool of water. The pup soaks up whatever you show him and constantly looks for more things to do and learn. At this early age, his body is not yet producing hormones, and therein lies the reason for such an high rate of success. Without hormones, he is focused on his owners and not

**REAP THE REWARDS**
If you start with a normal, healthy dog and give him time, patience and some carefully executed lessons, you will reap the rewards of that training for the life of the dog. And what a life it will be! The two of you will find immeasurable pleasure in the companionship you have built together with love, respect and understanding.

particularly interested in investigating other places, dogs, people, etc. You are his leader: his provider of food, water, shelter and security. He latches onto you and wants to stay close. He will usually follow you from room to room, will not let you out of his sight when you are outdoors with him and will respond in like manner to the people and animals you encounter. If you greet a friend warmly, he will be happy to greet the person as well. If, however, you are hesitant or anxious about the approach of a stranger, he will respond accordingly.

Once the puppy begins to produce hormones, his natural curiosity emerges and he begins to investigate the world around him. It is at this time when you may notice that the untrained dog begins to wander away from you and even ignore your commands to stay close. When this behaviour becomes a problem, you have two choices: get rid of the dog or train him. It is strongly urged that you choose the latter option.

You usually will be able to find obedience classes within a reasonable distance from your home, but you can also do a lot to train your dog yourself. Sometimes there are classes available, but the tuition is too costly. Whatever the circumstances, the solution to training your dog without obedience classes lies within the pages of this book.

This chapter is devoted to helping you train your Irish Red and White Setter at home. If the recommended procedures are followed faithfully, you may expect positive results that will prove rewarding both to you and your dog.

Whether your new charge is a puppy or a mature adult, the methods of teaching and the

### PARENTAL GUIDANCE

Training a dog is a life experience. Many parents admit that much of what they know about raising children they learned from caring for their dogs. Dogs respond to love, fairness and guidance, just as children do. Become a good dog owner and you may become an even better parent.

techniques we use in training basic behaviours are the same. After all, no dog, whether puppy or adult, likes harsh or inhumane methods. All creatures, however, respond favourably to gentle motivational methods and sincere praise and encouragement; this being particularly so with the Irish Red and White Setter, who thrives on positive reinforcement and does not respond well to punishment. Now let us get started.

## HOUSE-TRAINING

You can train a puppy to relieve himself wherever you choose, but this must be somewhere suitable. You should bear in mind from the outset that when your puppy is old enough to go out in public places, any canine deposits must be removed at once. You will always have to carry with you a small plastic bag or 'poop-scoop.'

Outdoor training includes such surfaces as grass, soil and cement. Indoor training usually means training your dog to newspaper. When deciding on the surface and location that you will want your Irish Red and White Setter to use, be sure it is going to be permanent. Training your dog to grass and then changing your mind a few months later is extremely difficult for both dog and owner.

Next, choose the command you will use each and every time

## MEALTIME
Mealtime should be a peaceful time for your dog. Do not put his food and water bowls in an high-traffic area in the house. For example, give him his own little corner of the kitchen where he can eat undisturbed and where he will not be underfoot. Do not allow small children or other family members to disturb the dog when he is eating.

you want your puppy to void. 'Hurry up' and 'Toilet' are examples of commands commonly used by dog owners. Get in the habit of giving the puppy your chosen relief command before you take him out. That way, when he becomes an adult, you will be able to determine if he wants to go out when you ask him. A confirmation will be signs of interest, wagging his tail, watching you intently, going to the door, etc.

### PUPPY'S NEEDS

Puppy needs to relieve himself after play periods, after each meal, after he has been sleeping and at any time he indicates that he is looking for a place to urinate or defecate. The urinary and intestinal tract muscles of very young puppies are not fully developed. Therefore, like human babies, puppies need to relieve themselves frequently.

Take your puppy out often—every hour for an eight-week-old, for example—and always immediately after sleeping and eating. The older the puppy, the less often he will need to relieve himself. Finally, as a mature healthy adult, he will require only three to five relief trips per day.

### HOUSING

Since the types of housing and control you provide for your puppy have a direct relationship on the success of house-training, we consider the various aspects of both before we begin training.

Taking a new puppy home and turning him loose in your house can be compared to turning a child loose in a sports arena and telling the child that the place is all his! The sheer enormity of the place would be too much for him to handle. Instead, offer the puppy clearly defined areas where he can play, sleep, eat and live. A room of the house where the family gathers is the most obvious choice. Puppies are social animals and need to feel a part of the pack right from the start. Hearing your voice, watching you while you are doing things and smelling you nearby are all positive reinforcers that he is now a member of your pack. Usually a family room, the kitchen or a nearby adjoining breakfast area is ideal for providing safety and security for both puppy and owner.

Within the designated room,

**THINK BEFORE YOU BARK**

Dogs are sensitive to their masters' moods and emotions. Use your voice wisely when communicating with your dog. Never raise your voice at your dog unless you are angry and trying to correct him. 'Barking' at your dog can become as meaningless as 'dogspeak' is to you. Think before you bark!

Containing the Red and White's enthusiasm requires high fencing! The gate that once kept the puppy within its confines may no longer be suitable for your ever-growing Red and White adult.

there should be a smaller area that the puppy can call his own. An alcove, a wire or fibreglass dog crate or a fenced (not boarded!) corner from which he can view the activities of his new family will be fine. The size of the area or crate is the key factor here. The area must be large enough so that the puppy can lie down and

### TAKE THE LEAD
Do not carry your dog to his toilet area. Lead him there on a leash or, better yet, encourage him to follow you to the spot. If you start carrying him to his spot, you might end up doing this routine forever and your dog will have the satisfaction of having trained YOU.

stretch out, as well as stand up, without rubbing his head on the top. At the same time, it must be small enough so that he cannot relieve himself at one end and sleep at the other without coming into contact with his droppings before he is fully trained to relieve himself outside. Dogs are, by nature, clean animals and will not remain close to their relief areas unless forced to do so. In those cases, they then become dirty dogs and usually remain that way for life.

The dog's designated area should contain clean bedding and a toy. Water must always be available, in a non-spill container, once house-training has been achieved reliably.

## HOUSE-TRAINING TIP

Most of all, be consistent. Always take your dog to the same location, always use the same command and always have the dog on lead when he is in his relief area, unless a fenced-in garden is available.

By following the Success Method, your puppy will be completely house-trained by the time his muscle and brain development reach maturity. Keep in mind that small breeds usually mature faster than large breeds, but all puppies should be trained by six months of age.

### CONTROL

By control, we mean helping the puppy to create a lifestyle pattern that will be compatible to that of his human pack (YOU!). Just as we guide little children to learn our way of life, we must show the puppy when it is time to play, eat, sleep, exercise and even entertain himself.

Your puppy should always sleep in his crate. He should also learn that, during times of household confusion and excessive human activity, such as at breakfast when family members are preparing for the day, he can play by himself in relative safety and comfort in his designated area. Each time you leave the puppy alone, he should understand exactly where he is to stay.

Puppies are chewers. They cannot tell the difference between lamp cords, television wires, shoes, table legs, etc. Chewing into a television wire, for example, can be fatal to the puppy, while a shorted wire can start a fire in the house. If the puppy chews on the arm of the chair when he is alone, you will probably discipline him angrily when you get home. Thus, he makes the association that your coming home means he is going to be punished. (He will not remember chewing the chair and is incapable of making the association of the discipline with his naughty deed.) Accustoming the pup to his designated area not only keeps him safe but also avoids his engaging in destructive behaviours when you are not around.

Times of excitement, such as special occasions, family parties, etc., can be fun for the puppy, providing that he can view the activities from the security of his designated area. He is not

# CANINE DEVELOPMENT SCHEDULE

It is important to understand how and at what age a puppy develops into adulthood. If you are a puppy owner, consult the following Canine Development Schedule to determine the stage of development your puppy is currently experiencing. This knowledge will help you as you work with the puppy in the weeks and months ahead.

| Period | Age | Characteristics |
|---|---|---|
| FIRST TO THIRD | BIRTH TO SEVEN WEEKS | Puppy needs food, sleep and warmth, and responds to simple and gentle touching. Needs mother for security and disciplining. Needs littermates for learning and interacting with other dogs. Pup learns to function within a pack and learns pack order of dominance. Begin socialising with adults and children for short periods. Begins to become aware of its environment. |
| FOURTH | EIGHT TO TWELVE WEEKS | Brain is fully developed. Needs socialising with outside world. Remove from mother and littermates. Needs to change from canine pack to human pack. Human dominance necessary. Fear period occurs between 8 and 12 weeks. Avoid fright and pain. |
| FIFTH | THIRTEEN TO SIXTEEN WEEKS | Training and formal obedience should begin. Less association with other dogs, more with people, places, situations. Period will pass easily if you remember this is pup's change-to-adolescence time. Be firm and fair. Flight instinct prominent. Permissiveness and over-disciplining can do permanent damage. Praise for good behaviour. |
| JUVENILE | FOUR TO EIGHT MONTHS | Another fear period about 7 to 8 months of age. It passes quickly, but be cautious of fright and pain. Sexual maturity reached. Dominant traits established. Dog should understand sit, down, come and stay by now. |

NOTE: THESE ARE APPROXIMATE TIME FRAMES. ALLOW FOR INDIVIDUAL DIFFERENCES IN PUPPIES.

underfoot and he is not being fed all sorts of titbits that will probably cause him stomach distress, yet he still feels a part of the fun.

SCHEDULE

A puppy should be taken to his relief area each time he is released from his designated area, after meals, after a play session and when he first awakens in the

**THE SUCCESS METHOD**
Success that comes by luck is usually short-lived. Success that comes by well-thought-out proven methods is often more easily achieved and permanent. This is the Success Method. It is designed to give you, the puppy owner, a simple yet proven way to help your puppy develop clean living habits and a feeling of security in his new environment.

**COMMAND STANCE**
Stand up straight and authoritatively when giving your dog commands. Do not issue commands when lying on the floor or lying on your back on the sofa. If you are on your hands and knees when you give a command, your dog will think you are positioning yourself to play.

morning (at age eight weeks, this can mean 5 a.m.!). The puppy will indicate that he's ready 'to go' by circling or sniffing busily—do not misinterpret these signs. For a puppy less than ten weeks of age, a routine of taking him out every hour is necessary. As the puppy grows, he will be able to wait for longer periods of time.

Keep trips to his relief area short. Stay no more than five or six minutes and then return to the house. If he goes during that time, praise him lavishly and take him indoors immediately. If he does not, but he has an accident when you go back indoors, pick him up immediately, say 'No! No!' and return to his relief area. Wait a few minutes, then return to the house again. Never hit a puppy or rub his face in urine or excrement when he has had an accident!

Once indoors, put the puppy in his crate until you have had time to clean up his accident.

## HOW MANY TIMES A DAY?

| AGE | RELIEF TRIPS |
|---|---|
| To 14 weeks | 10 |
| 14–22 weeks | 8 |
| 22–32 weeks | 6 |
| Adulthood | 4 |
| (dog stops growing) | |

These are estimates, of course, but they are a guide to the MINIMUM opportunities a dog should have each day to relieve itself.

Then, release him to the family area and watch him more closely than before. Chances are, his accident was a result of your not picking up his signal or waiting too long before offering him the opportunity to relieve himself. Never hold a grudge against the puppy for accidents.

Let the puppy learn that going outdoors means it is time to relieve himself, not to play. Once trained, he will be able to play indoors and out and still differentiate between the times for play versus the times for relief.

Help him develop regular hours for naps, being alone, playing by himself and just resting, all in his crate. Encourage him to entertain himself while you are busy with your activities. Let him learn that having you near is comforting, but it is not your main purpose in life to provide him with undivided attention.

Each time you put your puppy in his own area, use the same command, whatever suits best.

**Your Red and White will use his nose to locate his relief area. Once house-trained, he will consistently seek out the same area.**

## THE CLEAN LIFE

By providing sleeping and resting quarters that fit the dog, and offering frequent opportunities to relieve himself outside his quarters, the puppy quickly learns that the outdoors (or the newspaper if you are training him to paper) is the place to go when he needs to urinate or defecate. It also reinforces his innate desire to keep his sleeping quarters clean. This, in turn, helps develop the muscle control that will eventually produce a dog with clean living habits.

Soon he will run to his crate or special area when he hears you say those words.

Crate training provides safety for you, the puppy and the home. It also provides the puppy with a feeling of security, and that helps the puppy achieve self-confidence and clean habits. Remember that one of the primary ingredients in house-training your puppy is control.

Regardless of your lifestyle, there will always be occasions when you will need to have a place where your dog can stay and be happy and safe. Crate training is the answer for now and in the future.

In conclusion, a few key elements are really all you need for a successful house-training method—consistency, frequency, praise, control and supervision.

# THE SUCCESS METHOD

## 6 Steps to Successful Crate Training

**1** Tell the puppy 'Crate time!' and place him in the crate with a small treat (a piece of cheese or half of a biscuit). Let him stay in the crate for five minutes while you are in the same room. Then release him and praise lavishly. Never release him when he is fussing. Wait until he is quiet before you let him out.

**2** Repeat Step 1 several times a day.

**3** The next day, place the puppy in the crate as before. Let him stay there for ten minutes. Do this several times.

**4** Continue building time in five-minute increments until the puppy stays in his crate for 30 minutes with you in the room. Always take him to his relief area after prolonged periods in his crate.

**5** Now go back to Step 1 and let the puppy stay in his crate for five minutes, this time while you are out of the room.

**6** Once again, build crate time in five-minute increments with you out of the room. When the puppy will stay willingly in his crate (he may even fall asleep!) for 30 minutes with you out of the room, he will be ready to stay in it for several hours at a time.

## HONOUR AND OBEY

Dogs are the most honourable animals in existence. They consider another species (humans) as their own. They interface with you. You are their leader. Puppies perceive children to be on their level; their actions around small children are different from their behaviour around their adult masters.

By following these procedures with a normal, healthy puppy, you and the puppy will soon be past the stage of 'accidents' and ready to move on to a full and rewarding life together.

## ROLES OF DISCIPLINE, REWARD AND PUNISHMENT

Discipline, training one to act in accordance with rules, brings order to life. It is as simple as that. Without discipline, particularly in a group society, chaos will reign supreme and the group will eventually perish. Humans and canines are social animals and need some form of discipline in order to function effectively. They must procure food, protect their home base and their young and reproduce to keep their species going. If there were no discipline in the lives of social animals, they would eventually die from starvation and/or predation by other stronger animals.

In the case of domestic canines, discipline in their lives is needed in order for them to

## THE GOLDEN RULE

The golden rule of dog training is simple. For each 'question' (command), there is only one correct answer (reaction). One command = one reaction. Keep practising the command until the dog reacts correctly without hesitating. Be repetitive but not monotonous. Dogs get bored just as people do!

## TRAINING TIP

Dogs will do anything for your attention. If you reward the dog when he is calm and resting, you will develop a well-mannered dog. If, on the other hand, you greet your dog excitedly and encourage him to wrestle with you, the dog will greet you the same way and you will have an hyperactive dog on your hands.

A male's urge to lift his leg on every vertical surface he finds can be all-consuming. Curb your male's desire to have a wee on every possible upright object when he is still a puppy.

## FEAR AGGRESSION

Pups who are subjected to physical abuse during training commonly end up with behavioural problems as adults. One common result of abuse is fear aggression, in which a dog will lash out, bare his teeth, snarl and finally bite someone by whom he feels threatened. For example, your daughter may be playing with the dog one afternoon. As they play hide-and-seek, she backs the dog into a corner and, as she attempts to tease him playfully, he bites her hand. Examine the cause of this behaviour. Did your daughter ever hit the dog? Did someone who resembles your daughter hit or scream at the dog?

Fortunately, fear aggression is relatively easy to correct. Have your daughter engage in only positive activities with the dog, such as feeding, petting and walking. She should not give any corrections or negative feedback. If the dog still growls or cowers away from her, allow someone else to accompany them. After approximately one week, the dog should feel that he can rely on her for many positive things, and he will also be prevented from reacting fearfully towards anyone who might resemble her.

understand how their pack (you and other family members) functions and how they must act in order to survive.

A large humane society in an highly populated area recently surveyed dog owners regarding their satisfaction with their relationships with their dogs. People who had trained their dogs were 75% more satisfied with their pets than those who had never trained their dogs.

Dr Edward Thorndike, a psychologist, established *Thorndike's Theory of Learning*, which states that a behaviour that results in a pleasant event tends to be repeated. A behaviour that results in an unpleasant event tends not to be repeated. It is this theory upon which training methods are based today. For example, if you manipulate a dog to perform a specific behaviour and reward him for doing it, he is likely to do it again because he enjoyed the end result.

Occasionally, punishment, a penalty inflicted for an offence, is necessary. The best type of punishment often comes from an outside source. For example, a child is told not to touch the stove because he may get burned. He disobeys and touches the stove. In doing so, he receives a burn. From that time on, he respects the heat of the stove and avoids contact with it. Therefore, a behaviour that results in an unpleasant event tends not to be repeated.

A good example of a dog's learning the hard way is the dog who chases the house cat. He is told many times to leave the cat

## SAFETY FIRST

While it may seem that the most important things to your dog are eating, sleeping and chewing the upholstery on your furniture, his first concern is actually safety. The domesticated dogs we keep as companions have the same pack instinct as their ancestors who ran free thousands of years ago. Because of this pack instinct, your dog wants to know that he and his pack are not in danger of being harmed, and that his pack has a strong, capable leader. You must establish yourself as the leader early on in your relationship. That way your dog will trust that you will take care of him and the pack, and he will accept your commands without question.

not too heavy for the dog and perfectly safe.

### TREATS

Have a bag of treats on hand; something nutritious and easy to swallow works best. Use a soft treat, a chunk of cheese or a piece of cooked chicken rather than a dry biscuit. By the time the dog has finished chewing a dry treat, he will forget why he is being rewarded in the first place!

Using food rewards will not teach a dog to beg at the table—the only way to teach a dog to beg at the table is to give him food from the table. In training, rewarding the dog with a food treat will help him associate praise and the treats with learning new behaviours that obviously please his owner.

### TRAINING BEGINS: ASK THE DOG A QUESTION

In order to teach your dog anything, you must first get his attention. After all, he cannot learn anything if he is looking away from you with his mind on something else.

alone, yet he persists in teasing the cat. Then, one day, the dog begins chasing the cat but the cat turns and swipes a claw across the dog's face, leaving the dog with a painful gash on his nose. The final result is that the dog stops chasing the cat. Again, a behaviour that results in an unpleasant event tends not to be repeated.

## TRAINING EQUIPMENT

### COLLAR AND LEAD

For an Irish Red and White Setter, the collar and lead that you use for training must be one with which you are easily able to work,

Clean up after your dog has relieved itself, even in your own garden. You can purchase a tool to make the task more manageable.

To get your dog's attention, ask him 'School?' and immediately walk over to him and give him a treat as you tell him 'Good dog.' Wait a minute or two and repeat the routine, this time with a treat in your hand as you approach within a foot of the dog. Do not go directly to him, but stop about a foot short of him and hold out the treat as you ask 'School?' He will see you approaching with a treat in your hand and most likely begin walking toward you. As you meet, give him the treat and praise again.

The third time, ask the question, have a treat in your hand and walk only a short distance toward the dog so that he must walk almost all the way to you. As he reaches you, give him the treat and praise again.

*All members of the family should take part in the Red and White's training so that he will behave politely and obey commands no matter with whom he's spending time.*

**ATTENTION!**
Your dog is actually training you at the same time you are training him. Dogs do things to get attention. They usually repeat whatever succeeds in getting your attention.

By this time, the dog will probably be getting the idea that if he pays attention to you, especially when you ask that question, it will pay off in treats and enjoyable activities for him. In other words, he learns that 'school' means doing great things with you that are fun and that result in positive attention for him.

Remember that the dog does not understand your verbal language; he only recognises sounds. Your question translates

**PLAN TO PLAY**
The puppy should also have regular play and exercise sessions when he is with you or a family member. Exercise for a very young puppy can consist of a short walk around the house or garden. Playing can include fetching games with a large ball or a special raggy. (All puppies teethe and need soft things upon which to chew.) Remember to restrict play periods to indoors within his living area (the family room, for example) until he is completely house-trained.

to a series of sounds for him, and those sounds become the signal to go to you and pay attention. The dog learns that if he does this, he will get to interact with you plus receive treats and praise.

## THE BASIC COMMANDS

### TEACHING SIT

Now that you have the dog's attention, attach his lead and hold it in your left hand, and hold a food treat in your right hand. Place your food hand at the dog's nose and let him lick the treat but not take it from you. Say 'Sit' and slowly raise your food hand from in front of the dog's nose up over his head so that he is looking at the ceiling. As he bends his head upward, he will have to bend his knees to maintain his balance. As he bends his knees, he will assume a sit position. At that point, release the food treat and praise

## TRAINING RULES

If you want to be successful in training your dog, you have four rules to obey yourself:

1. Develop an understanding of how a dog thinks.
2. Do not blame the dog for lack of communication.
3. Define your dog's personality and act accordingly.
4. Have patience and be consistent.

lavishly with comments such as 'Good dog! Good sit!,' etc. Remember to always praise enthusiastically, because dogs relish verbal praise from their owners and feel so proud of themselves whenever they accomplish a behaviour.

You will not use food forever in getting the dog to obey your commands. Food is only used to teach new behaviours and, once

**You must have your Red and White's attention before beginning a training session. Ask him 'School?' to get his attention, and then proceed with the lesson as planned.**

when you say 'Down' or he attempts to snap at the person who tries to force him down.

Have the dog sit close alongside your left leg, facing in the same direction as you are. Hold the lead in your left hand and a food treat in your right. Now place your left hand lightly on the top of the dog's shoulders where they meet above the spinal cord. Do not push down on the dog's shoulders; simply rest your left hand there so you can guide the dog to lie down close to your left leg rather than

*The sit exercise is commonly the first lesson introduced to the canine student. You may need to guide your Red and White into the position a few times to show him what is expected.*

the dog knows what you want when you give a specific command, you will wean him off the food treats but still maintain the verbal praise. After all, you will always have your voice with you, and there will be many times when you have no food rewards but expect the dog to obey.

## TEACHING DOWN

Teaching the down exercise is easy when you understand how the dog perceives the down position, and it is very difficult when you do not. Dogs perceive the down position as a submissive one; therefore, teaching the down exercise by using a forceful method can sometimes make the dog develop such a fear of the down that he either runs away

## THE STUDENT'S STRESS TEST

During training sessions you must be able to recognise signs of stress in your dog such as:
- tucking his tail between his legs
- lowering his head
- shivering or trembling
- standing completely still or running away
- panting and/or salivating
- avoiding eye contact
- flattening his ears back
- urinating submissively
- rolling over and lifting a leg
- grinning or baring teeth
- aggression when restrained

If your four-legged student displays these signs, he may just be nervous or intimidated. The training session may have been too lengthy, with not enough praise and affirmation. Stop for the day and try again tomorrow.

to swing away from your side when he drops.

Now place the food hand at the dog's nose, say 'Down' very softly (almost a whisper), and slowly lower the food hand to the dog's front feet. When the food hand reaches the floor, begin moving it forward along the floor in front of the dog. Keep talking softly to the dog, saying things like, 'Do you want this treat? You can do this, good dog.' Your reassuring tone of voice will help calm the dog as he tries to follow the food hand in order to get the treat.

When the dog's elbows touch the floor, release the food and praise softly. Try to get the dog to maintain that down position for several seconds before you let him sit up again. The goal here is to get the dog to settle down and not feel threatened in the down position.

### TEACHING STAY

It is easy to teach the dog to stay in either a sit or a down position. Again, we use food and praise during the teaching process as we help the dog to understand exactly what it is that we are expecting him to do.

To teach the sit/stay, start with the dog sitting on your left side as before and hold the lead in your left hand. Have a food treat in your right hand and place your food hand at the dog's nose. Say

'Stay' and step out on your right foot to stand directly in front of the dog, toe to toe, as he licks and nibbles the treat. Be sure to keep his head facing upward to maintain the sit position. Count to five and then swing around to stand next to the dog again with him on your left. As soon as you

**DOUBLE JEOPARDY**
A dog in jeopardy never lies down. He stays alert on his feet because instinct tells him that he may have to run away or fight for his survival. Therefore, if a dog feels threatened or anxious, he will not lie down. Consequently, it is important to have the dog calm and relaxed as he learns the down exercise.

get back to the original position, release the food and praise lavishly.

To teach the down/stay, do the down as previously described. As soon as the dog lies down, say 'Stay' and step out on your right foot just as you did in the sit/stay. Count to five and then return to stand beside the dog with him on your left side. Release the treat and praise as always.

Within a week or ten days, you can begin to add a bit of distance between you and your dog when you leave him. When you do, use your left hand open with the palm facing the dog as a stay signal, much the same as the hand signal a constable uses to stop traffic at a juncture. Hold the food treat in your right hand as before, but this time the food will not be touching the dog's nose. He will watch the food hand and quickly learn that he is

**CONSISTENCY PAYS OFF**
Dogs need consistency in their feeding schedule, exercise and toilet breaks, and in the verbal commands you use. If you use 'Stay' on Monday and 'Stay here, please' on Tuesday, you will confuse your dog. Don't demand perfect behaviour during training classes and then let him have the run of the house the rest of the day. Above all, lavish praise on your pet consistently every time he does something right. The more he feels he is pleasing you, the more willing he will be to learn.

going to get that treat as soon as you return to his side.

When you can stand 1 metre away from your dog for 30 seconds, you can then begin building time and distance in both stays. Eventually, the dog can be expected to remain in the stay position for prolonged periods of time until you return to him or call him to you. Always praise lavishly when he stays.

TEACHING COME
If you make teaching 'come' an exciting experience, you should never have a 'student' that does not love the game or that fails to come when called. The secret, it seems, is never to teach the word 'come.'

At times when an owner most wants his dog to come when

To teach the down/stay, step out in front of the dog while maintaining the hand signal for 'stay.'

called, the owner is likely to be upset or anxious and he allows these feelings to come through in the tone of his voice when he calls his dog. Hearing that desperation in his owner's voice, the dog fears the results of going to him and therefore either disobeys outright or runs in the opposite direction. The secret, therefore, is to teach the dog a game and, when you want him to come to you, simply play the game. It is practically a no-fail solution!

To begin, have several members of your family take a few food treats and each go into a different room in the house. Everyone takes turns calling the dog, and each person should celebrate the dog's finding him with a treat and lots of happy praise. When a person calls the dog, he is actually inviting the dog to find him and to get a treat as a reward for 'winning.'

A few turns of the 'Where are you?' game and the dog will

The trainer's arms outstretched signal that the dog is released from the 'stay' and should 'come' to the trainer.

understand that everyone is playing the game and that each person has a big celebration awaiting the dog's success at locating him or her. Once the dog learns to love the game, simply calling out 'Where are you?' will bring him running from wherever he is when he hears that all-important question.

The come command is recognised as one of the most important things to teach a dog, but there are trainers who work with thousands of dogs and never teach the actual word 'come.' Yet these dogs will race to respond to a person who uses the dog's name followed by 'Where are you?' For example, a woman has a 12-year-old companion dog who went blind, but who never fails to locate her owner when asked, 'Where are you?'

Children, in particular, love to play this game with their dogs. Children can hide in smaller places like a shower or bath, behind a bed or under a table. The dog needs to work a little bit

---

## 'WHERE ARE YOU?'

When calling the dog, do not say 'Come.' Say things like, 'Rover, where are you? See if you can find me! I have a biscuit for you!' Keep up a constant line of chatter with coaxing sounds and frequent questions such as, 'Where are you?' The dog will learn to follow the sound of your voice to locate you and receive his reward.

Limit the distractions in your training area. If your Red and White is gazing far afield, his attention is nowhere near the lesson at hand.

harder to find these hiding places, but, when he does, he loves to celebrate with a treat and a tussle with a favourite youngster.

### TEACHING HEEL

Heeling means that the dog walks beside the owner without pulling. It takes time and patience on the owner's part to succeed at teaching the dog that he (the owner) will not proceed unless the dog is walking calmly beside him. Neither pulling out ahead on the lead nor lagging behind is acceptable.

Begin by holding the lead in your left hand as the dog sits beside your left leg. Move the loop end of the lead to your right hand, but keep your left hand short on the lead so that it keeps the dog in close next to you.

Say 'Heel' and step forward on your left foot. Keep the dog close to you and take three steps. Stop and have the dog sit next to you in what we now call the 'heel position.' Praise verbally, but do not touch the dog. Hesitate a

moment and begin again with 'Heel,' taking three steps and stopping, at which point the dog is told to sit again.

Your goal here is to have the dog walk those three steps without pulling on the lead. Once he will walk calmly beside you for three steps without pulling, increase the number of steps you take to five. When he will walk politely beside you while you take five steps, you can increase the length of your walk to ten steps. Keep increasing the length of your stroll until the dog will walk quietly beside you without pulling as long as you want him to heel. When you stop heeling, indicate to the dog that the exercise is over by verbally praising as you pet him and say 'OK, good dog.' The 'OK' is used as a release word, meaning that the exercise is finished and the dog is free to relax.

If you are dealing with a dog who insists on pulling you

---

### 'COME' . . . BACK

Never call your dog to come to you for a correction or scold him when he reaches you. That is the quickest way to turn a 'Come' command into 'Go away fast!' Dogs think only in the present tense, and your dog will connect the scolding with coming to you, not with the misbehaviour of a few moments earlier.

Heeling is a vital lesson to teach a dog as large as the Red and White, or else daily walks would be quite a chore. The dog should walk by his owner's left side without pulling ahead, keeping pace with his owner the whole time.

During the heeling lesson, the dog only walks as many steps as the owner indicates, learning that the owner controls how fast and far the pair will travel.

Each time the dog looks up at you or slows down to give a slack lead between the two of you, quietly praise him and say, 'Good heel. Good dog.' Eventually, the dog will begin to respond and within a few days he will be walking politely beside you without pulling on the lead. At first, the training sessions should be kept short and very positive; soon the dog will be able to walk nicely with you for increasingly longer distances. Remember also to give the dog free time and the opportunity to run and play when you have finished heel practice.

## WEANING OFF FOOD IN TRAINING

Food is used in training new behaviours. Once the dog understands what behaviour goes with a specific command, it is time to start weaning him off the food treats. At first, give a treat after each exercise. Then, start to give a treat only after every other exercise. Mix up the times when you offer a food reward and the

around, simply 'put on your brakes' and stand your ground until the dog realises that the two of you are not going anywhere until he is beside you and moving at your pace, not his. It may take some time just standing there to convince the dog that you are the leader and that you will be the one to decide on the direction and speed of your travel.

---

**TUG OF WALK?**

If you begin teaching the heel by taking long walks and letting the dog pull you along, he misinterprets this action as an acceptable form of taking a walk. When you pull back on the lead to counteract his pulling, he reads that tug as a signal to pull even harder!

times when you only offer praise so that the dog will never know when he is going to receive both food and praise and when he is going to receive only praise. This is called a variable ratio reward system. It proves successful because there is always the chance that the owner will produce a treat, so the dog never stops trying for that reward. No matter what, always give verbal praise.

## OBEDIENCE CLASSES

It is a good idea to enrol in an obedience class if one is available in your area. If yours is a show dog, ringcraft classes would be more appropriate. Many areas have dog clubs that offer basic obedience training as well as preparatory classes for obedience competition. There are also local dog trainers who offer similar classes.

## TRAINING TIP

If you are walking your dog and he suddenly stops and looks straight into your eyes, ignore him. Pull the leash and lead him into the direction you want to walk.

## OBEDIENCE SCHOOL

A basic obedience beginner's class usually lasts for six to eight weeks. Dog and owner attend an hour-long lesson once a week and practise for a few minutes, several times a day, each day at home. If done properly, the whole procedure will result in a well-mannered dog and an owner who delights in living with a pet that is eager to please and enjoys doing things with his owner.

At obedience shows, dogs can earn titles at various levels of competition. The beginning levels of obedience competition include basic behaviours such as sit, down, heel, etc. The more advanced levels of competition include jumping, retrieving, scent discrimination and signal work. The advanced levels require a dog and owner to put a lot of time and effort into their training. The titles that can be earned at these levels of competition are very prestigious.

## OTHER ACTIVITIES FOR LIFE

Whether a dog is trained in the structured environment of a class

## HOW TO WEAN THE 'TREAT HOG'

If you have trained your dog by rewarding him with a treat each time he performs a command, he may soon decide that without the treat, he won't sit, stay or come. The best way to fix this problem is to start asking your dog to do certain commands twice before being rewarded. Slowly increase the number of commands given and then vary the number: three sits and a treat one day, five sits for a biscuit the next day, etc. Your dog will soon realise that there is no set number of sits before he gets his reward, and he'll likely do it the first time you ask in the hope of being rewarded sooner rather than later.

## HELPING PAWS

Your dog may not be the next Lassie, but every pet has the potential to do some tricks well. Identify his natural talents and hone them. Is your dog always happy and upbeat? Teach him to wag his tail or give you his paw on command. Real homebodies can be trained to do household chores, such as carrying dirty washing or retrieving the morning paper.

or alone with his owner at home, there are many activities that can bring fun and rewards to both owner and dog once they have mastered basic control.

Teaching the dog to help out around the home, in the garden or on the farm provides great satisfaction to both dog and owner. In addition, the dog's help makes life a little easier for his owner and raises his stature as a valued companion to his family. It helps give the dog a purpose by occupying his mind and providing an outlet for his energy.

Backpacking is an exciting and healthy activity that the dog can be taught without assistance from more than his owner. The exercise of walking and climbing is good for man and dog alike, and the bond that they develop together is priceless. The rule for backpacking with any dog is never to expect the dog to carry

more than one-sixth of his body weight.

If you are interested in participating in organised competition with your Irish Red and White Setter, there are activities other than obedience in which you and your dog can become involved. Because the Irish Red and White was bred to be an hunting dog, your dog will enjoy the chance to use his natural instincts in organised events. Breed clubs can give you information about field work, hunting events and related activities, whether competitive or just for fun, in which you can participate with your Red and White.

Agility is a popular sport in which dogs run through an obstacle course that includes various jumps, tunnels and other

## PRACTICE MAKES PERFECT!

- Have training lessons with your dog every day in several short segments—three to five times a day for a few minutes at a time is ideal.
- Do not have long practice sessions. The dog will become easily bored.
- Never practise when you are tired, ill, worried or in an otherwise negative mood. This will transmit to the dog and may have an adverse effect on its performance.

Think fun, short and above all POSITIVE! End each session on an high note, rather than a failed exercise, and make sure to give a lot of praise. Enjoy the training and help your dog enjoy it, too.

## NATURAL PRODIGY

Occasionally, a dog and owner who have not attended formal classes have been able to earn entry-level titles by obtaining competition rules and regulations from a local kennel club and practising on their own to a degree of perfection. Obtaining the higher level titles, however, almost always requires extensive training under the tutelage of experienced instructors. In addition, the more difficult levels require more specialised equipment whereas the lower levels do not.

exercises to test the dog's speed and coordination. The owners run beside their dogs to give commands and to guide them through the course. Although competitive, the focus is on fun—it's fun to do, fun to watch and great exercise.

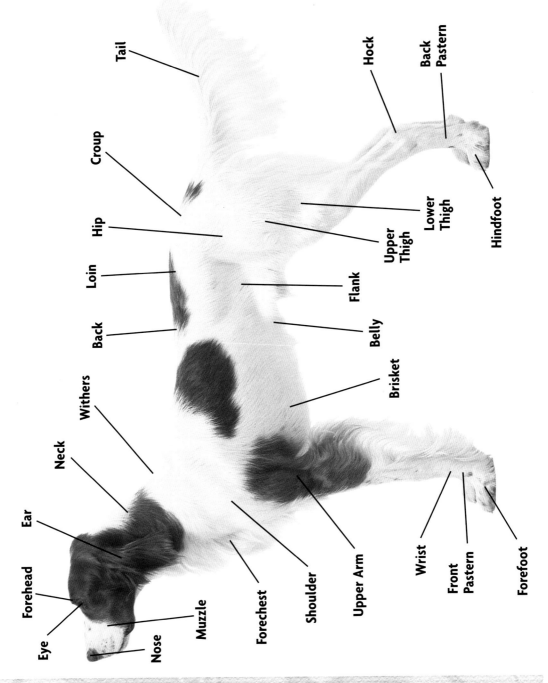

PHYSICAL STRUCTURE OF THE IRISH RED AND WHITE SETTER

Dogs suffer from many of the same physical illnesses as people. They might even share many of the same psychological problems. Since people usually know more about human diseases than canine maladies, many of the terms used in this chapter will be familiar but not necessarily those used by veterinary surgeons. For example, we will use the term *x-ray* instead of *radiograph*. We will also use the familiar term *symptoms*, even though dogs don't have symptoms, which are verbal descriptions of something the patient feels or observes himself that he regards as abnormal. Dogs have *clinical signs*; since dogs cannot speak, we have to look for these clinical signs...but we still use the term *symptoms* in the book.

Medicine is a constantly changing art, with some scientific input as well. Things alter as we learn more and more about basic sciences such as genetics and biochemistry, and have use of more sophisticated imaging techniques like Computer Aided Tomography (CAT scans) or Magnetic Resonance Imaging (MRI scans). There is academic dispute about many canine maladies, so different veterinary surgeons treat them in different ways, and some vets place a greater emphasis on surgical techniques than others.

## SELECTING A VETERINARY SURGEON
Your selection of a veterinary surgeon should be based on personal recommendation for their skills with small animals, especially dogs, and, if possible, especially gundogs. If the vet is based nearby, it will be helpful because you might have an emergency or need to make multiple visits for treatments.

All veterinary surgeons are licenced, and in Britain are Members of the Royal College of Veterinary Surgeons (MRCVS after their names). The high street veterinary practice deals with routine medical issues such as infections, injuries and the promotion of health (for example, by vaccination). If the problem affecting your dog is more complex, in Britain your vet will refer your pet to someone with a more detailed knowledge of what is wrong. This will usually be a specialist at the nearest university veterinary school who is a veterinary dermatologist, veterinary ophthalmologist, etc; whichever is the relevant field.

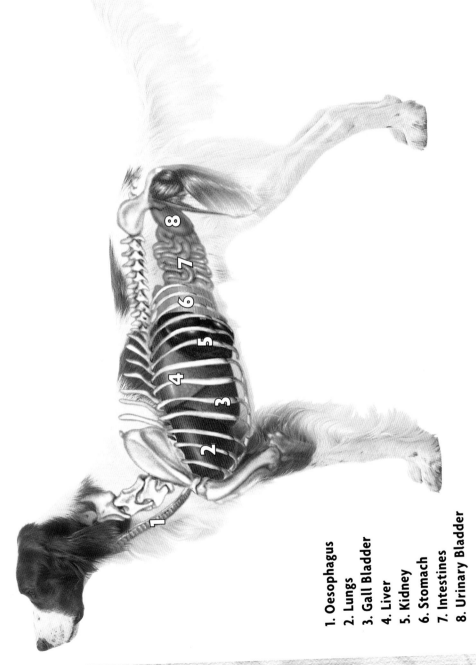

1. Oesophagus
2. Lungs
3. Gall Bladder
4. Liver
5. Kidney
6. Stomach
7. Intestines
8. Urinary Bladder

INTERNAL ORGANS OF THE IRISH RED AND WHITE SETTER

Veterinary procedures are very costly and as the treatments available improve, they are going to become more expensive. It is quite acceptable to discuss matters of cost with your vet; if there is more than one treatment option, cost may be a factor in deciding which route to take.

Insurance against veterinary cost is also becoming very popular. This will not pay for routine vaccinations, but will cover the costs for unexpected emergencies such as emergency surgery after a road traffic accident.

## PREVENTATIVE MEDICINE
It is much easier, less costly and more effective to practise preventative medicine than to fight bouts of illness and disease. Properly bred puppies of all breeds come

**Breakdown of Veterinary Income by Category**

| | |
|---|---|
| 2% | Dentistry |
| 4% | Radiology |
| 12% | Surgery |
| 15% | Vaccinations |
| 19% | Laboratory |
| 23% | Examinations |
| 25% | Medicines |

from parents that were selected based upon their genetic disease profile. Luckily, the Irish Red and White Setter is overall an hardy, healthy breed, with concentrated efforts being taken to eliminate the few hereditary diseases seen in the breed.

A typical American vet's income, categorised according to services performed. This survey dealt with small-animal (pets) practices.

## HOW TO PREVENT BLOAT
Research has confirmed that the structure of deep-chested breeds contributes to their predisposition to bloat/gastric dilatation. Therefore, every owner of an Irish Red and White should take the following precautions to reduce the risk of this potentially deadly condition:

- Divide the dog's daily food ration into two smaller meals, rather than feeding one large meal.
- Wait at least an hour after exercise before feeding your dog, and wait at least two hours after the dog has eaten before exercising him.
- Be sure that the dog is calm while he is eating. Research has proven that nervous, agitated or overly excited dogs are more prone to bloat.
- If you feed dried food, mix a small amount of moist food in with his portion of dried food.
- Elevate your dog's food and water bowls on stands; this will prevent his craning his neck to eat and drink, thus reducing the risk of his swallowing air (a major cause of bloat).
- To prevent your dog from gobbling his food too quickly, and thereby swallowing air, put some large (unswallowable) toys into his bowl so that he must work around them to get to his food.

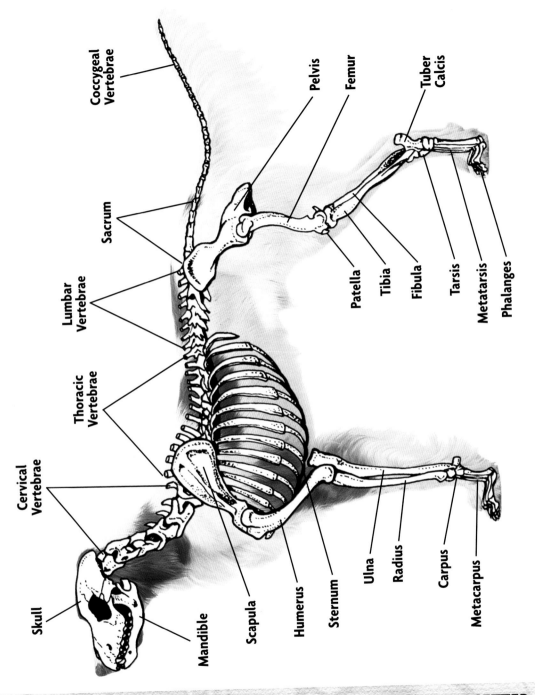

Coccygeal Vertebrae

Pelvis

Femur

Tuber Calcis

Sacrum

Patella

Tibia

Fibula

Tarsis

Metatarsis

Phalanges

Lumbar Vertebrae

Thoracic Vertebrae

Cervical Vertebrae

Skull

Mandible

Scapula

Humerus

Sternum

Ulna

Radius

Carpus

Metacarpus

SKELETAL STRUCTURE OF THE IRISH RED AND WHITE SETTER

The puppies' mother should have been vaccinated, free of all internal and external parasites and properly nourished. For these reasons, a visit to the veterinary surgeon who cared for the dam (mother) is recommended if at all possible. The dam passes disease resistance to her puppies, which should last from eight to ten weeks. Unfortunately, she can also pass on parasites and infection. This is why knowledge about her health is useful in learning more about the health of the puppies.

### WEANING TO FIVE MONTHS OLD
Puppies should be weaned by the time they are two months old. A puppy that remains for at least eight weeks with its mother and littermates usually adapts better to other dogs and people later in its life. Some new owners have their puppy examined by a veterinary surgeon immediately, which is a good idea unless the puppy is overtired by a long journey. Vaccination programmes usually begin when the puppy is very young.

The puppy will have its teeth examined and have its skeletal conformation and general health checked prior to certification by the veterinary surgeon. Puppies in certain breeds have problems with their kneecaps, cataracts and other

# HEALTH AND VACCINATION SCHEDULE

| AGE IN WEEKS: | 6TH | 8TH | 10TH | 12TH | 14TH | 16TH | 20-24TH | 52ND |
|---|---|---|---|---|---|---|---|---|
| Worm Control | ✔ | ✔ | ✔ | ✔ | ✔ | ✔ | ✔ | |
| Neutering | | | | | | | | ✔ |
| Heartworm | | ✔ | | ✔ | | ✔ | ✔ | |
| Parvovirus | ✔ | | ✔ | | ✔ | | ✔ | ✔ |
| Distemper | | ✔ | | ✔ | | ✔ | | ✔ |
| Hepatitis | | ✔ | | ✔ | | ✔ | | ✔ |
| Leptospirosis | | | | | | | | ✔ |
| Parainfluenza | ✔ | | ✔ | | ✔ | | | ✔ |
| Dental Examination | | ✔ | | | | | ✔ | ✔ |
| Complete Physical | | ✔ | | | | | ✔ | ✔ |
| Coronavirus | | | | ✔ | | | ✔ | ✔ |
| Kennel Cough | ✔ | | | | | | | |
| Hip Dysplasia | | | | | | | | ✔ |
| Rabies | | | | | | | ✔ | |

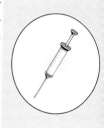

Vaccinations are not instantly effective. It takes about two weeks for the dog's immune system to develop antibodies. Most vaccinations require annual booster shots. Your veterinary surgeon should guide you in this regard.

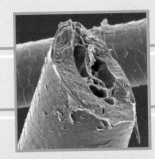

Normal hairs of a dog enlarged 200 times original size. The cuticle (outer covering) is clean and healthy. Unlike human hair that grows from the base, a dog's hair also grows from the end. Damaged hairs and split ends, illustrated above.

# DISEASE REFERENCE CHART

| | What is it? | What causes it? | Symptoms |
|---|---|---|---|
| **Leptospirosis** | Severe disease that affects the internal organs; can be spread to people. | A bacterium, which is often carried by rodents, that enters through mucous membranes and spreads quickly throughout the body. | Range from fever, vomiting and loss of appetite in less severe cases to shock, irreversible kidney damage and possibly death in most severe cases. |
| **Rabies** | Potentially deadly virus that infects warm-blooded mammals. Not seen in United Kingdom. | Bite from a carrier of the virus, mainly wild animals. | 1st stage: dog exhibits change in behaviour, fear. 2nd stage: dog's behaviour becomes more aggressive. 3rd stage: loss of coordination, trouble with bodily functions. |
| **Parvovirus** | Highly contagious virus, potentially deadly. | Ingestion of the virus, which is usually spread through the faeces of infected dogs. | Most common: severe diarrhoea. Also vomiting, fatigue, lack of appetite. |
| **Kennel cough** | Contagious respiratory infection. | Combination of types of bacteria and virus. Most common: *Bordetella bronchiseptica* bacteria and parainfluenza virus. | Chronic cough. |
| **Distemper** | Disease primarily affecting respiratory and nervous system. | Virus that is related to the human measles virus. | Mild symptoms such as fever, lack of appetite and mucous secretion progress to evidence of brain damage, 'hard pad.' |
| **Hepatitis** | Virus primarily affecting the liver. | Canine adenovirus type I (CAV-1). Enters system when dog breathes in particles. | Lesser symptoms include listlessness, diarrhoea, vomiting. More severe symptoms include 'blue-eye' (clumps of virus in eye). |
| **Coronavirus** | Virus resulting in digestive problems. | Virus is spread through infected dog's faeces. | Stomach upset evidenced by lack of appetite, vomiting, diarrhoea. |

eye problems, heart murmurs and undescended testicles. They may also have personality problems and your veterinary surgeon might have training in temperament evaluation.

## VACCINATION SCHEDULING

Most vaccinations are given by injection and should only be given by a veterinary surgeon. Both he and you should keep a record of the date of the injection, the identification of the vaccine and the amount given. Some vets give a first vaccination at eight weeks, but most dog breeders prefer the course not to commence until about ten weeks because of interaction with the antibodies produced by the mother.

The vaccination scheduling is usually based on a 15-day cycle. You must take your vet's advice as to when to vaccinate, as this may differ according to the vaccine used. The usual vaccines contain immunising doses of several different viruses such as distemper, parvovirus, parainfluenza and hepatitis. There are other vaccines available when the puppy is at risk. You should rely upon professional advice. This is especially true for the booster immunisations. Most vaccination programmes require a booster when the puppy is a year old and once a year thereafter. In some cases, circumstances may require more frequent immunisations.

Kennel cough, more formally known as tracheobronchitis, is immunised against with a vaccine that is sprayed into the dog's nostrils. Kennel cough is usually included in routine vaccination, but it is often not as effective as the vaccines for other major diseases.

### FIVE MONTHS TO ONE YEAR OF AGE

Unless you intend to breed from or show your dog, the general advice is to get your dog neutered (male) or spayed (female). Discuss this with your veterinary surgeon, as the procedure has proven to be extremely beneficial to both male and female puppies. Besides eliminating the possibility of pregnancy, it inhibits (but does not prevent) breast cancer in bitches and prostate cancer in male dogs. Under no circumstances should a bitch be spayed prior to her first season.

Your veterinary surgeon should provide your puppy with a thorough dental evaluation at six months of age, ascertaining whether all the permanent teeth have erupted properly. An home dental-care regimen should be initiated at six months, including brushing weekly and providing good dental devices (such as nylon bones). Regular dental care promotes healthy teeth, fresh breath and a longer life.

### DOGS OLDER THAN ONE YEAR

Continue to visit the veterinary surgeon at least once a year. There is no such disease as 'old age,' but bodily functions do change with age. The eyes and ears are no longer as efficient. Liver, kidney and intestinal functions often decline. Proper dietary changes, recommended by your veterinary surgeon, can make life more pleasant for your ageing Irish Red and White Setter and you.

### SKIN PROBLEMS

Veterinary surgeons are consulted by dog owners for skin problems more than for any other group of diseases or maladies. A dog's skin is as sensitive, if not more so, than human skin, and both suffer almost the same ailments (though the occurrence of acne in most dogs is rare!). For this reason, veterinary dermatology has developed into a speciality practised by many veterinary surgeons.

Since many skin problems have visual symptoms that are almost identical, it requires the skill of an experienced veterinary dermatologist to identify and cure many of the more severe skin disorders. Pet shops sell many treatments for skin problems but most of the treatments are directed at symptoms and not at the underlying problem(s). If your dog is suffering from a skin disorder, you should seek professional assistance as quickly as possible. As with all diseases, the earlier a problem is identified and treated, the more successful is the cure.

### PARASITE BITES

Many of us are allergic to insect bites. The bites itch, erupt and may even become infected. Dogs have the same reaction to fleas, ticks and/or mites. When an insect lands on you, you have the chance to whisk it away with your hand. Unfortunately, when a dog is bitten by a flea, tick or mite, it can only scratch it away or bite it. By the time the dog has been bitten, the parasite has done some of its damage. It may also have laid eggs, which will cause further problems in the near future. The itching from parasite bites is probably due to the saliva injected into the site when the parasite sucks the dog's blood.

### ACRAL LICK GRANULOMA

Many large dogs have a poorly understood condition called acral lick granuloma. The manifestation of the problem is the dog's tireless attack at a specific area of the body, almost always the legs or paws. The dog licks so intensively that he removes the hair and skin,

leaving an ugly large wound. Tiny protuberances, which are outgrowths of new capillaries, bead on the surface of the wound. Owners who notice their dogs' biting and chewing at their extremities should have the vet determine the cause. If lick granuloma is identified, although there is no absolute cure, corticosteroids are the most common treatment.

### AIRBORNE ALLERGIES

Just as humans have hay fever from which they suffer during the pollinating season, many dogs suffer from the same allergies.

A dog's skin is sensitive and can develop allergies and rashes. Be wary of what your puppy encounters when exploring the outdoors.

When the pollen count is high, your dog might suffer, but don't expect him to sneeze and have a runny nose as a human would. Dogs react to pollen allergies in the same way they react to fleas—they scratch and bite themselves.

Dogs, like humans, can be tested for allergens. Discuss the testing with your veterinary surgeon.

### AUTOIMMUNE ILLNESSES

An autoimmune illness is one in which the immune system overacts and does not recognise parts of the affected person (or dog); rather, the immune system starts to react as if these parts were foreign and need to be destroyed. An example is rheumatoid arthritis, which occurs when the body does not recognise the joints, thus leading to a very painful and damaging reaction in the joints. This has nothing to do with age, so can occur in children. The wear-and-tear arthritis of the older person or dog is osteoarthritis.

Lupus is an autoimmune disease that affects dogs as well as people. It can take variable forms, affecting the kidneys, bones and the skin. It can be fatal, so is treated with steroids, which can themselves have very significant side effects. The steroids calm down the allergic reaction to the body's tissues, which helps the lupus, but also calms down the body's reaction to real foreign substances such as bacteria, and also thins the skin and bone.

### FOOD PROBLEMS

#### FOOD ALLERGIES

Dogs are allergic to many foods that are best sellers and highly recommended by breeders and veterinary surgeons. Changing the brand of food that you buy may not eliminate the problem if the element to which the dog is allergic is contained in the new brand as well.

Recognising a food allergy can be difficult. Humans often have rashes when they eat foods to which they are allergic, or have swelling of the lips or eyes. Dogs do not usually develop rashes, but react in the same way as they do to an airborne or bite allergy—they itch, scratch and bite. While pollen allergies and parasite bites are usually seasonal, pollen allergies are year-round problems.

#### TREATING FOOD ALLERGY

Diagnosis of food allergy is based on a two- to four-week dietary trial with an home-cooked diet fed to the exclusion of all other foods. The diet should consist of boiled rice or potato with a source of protein that the dog has never eaten before, such as fresh or frozen fish, lamb or even something as exotic as pheasant. Water has to be the only drink,

## OTHER HEALTH ISSUES

The IRWSCGB has had two instances of von Willebrand's disease (vWD), a blood clotting disorder, but has now initiated a DNA test to deal with that. Also, there is no megaoesphagus in Irish Red and White—in spite of much asking.

and it is really important that no other foods are fed during this trial.

If the dog's condition improves, you will need to try the original diet once again to see if the itching resumes. If it does, then this confirms the diagnosis that the dog is allergic to its original diet. The treatment is long-term feeding of something that does not distress the dog's skin, which may be in the form of one of the commercially available hypoallergenic diets or the home-made diet that you created for the allergy trial.

### FOOD INTOLERANCE

Food intolerance is the inability of the dog to completely digest certain foods. This occurs because the dog does not have the chemicals necessary to digest some foodstuffs. These chemicals are called enzymes. All puppies have the enzymes necessary to digest canine milk, but some dogs do not have the enzymes to digest a very different form of milk that

is commonly found in human households—milk from cows. In such dogs, drinking cows' milk results in loose bowels, stomach pains and the passage of gas. These are the only obvious symptoms of food intolerance, which makes diagnosis difficult.

A change in diet, by eliminating certain ingredients in the dog's food and substituting with new ingredients that are not in the current diet, will eventually enable you to isolate the food ingredient to which your dog is intolerant.

## MANY KINDS OF EARS

Not every dog's ears are the same. Ears that are open to the air are healthier than ears with poor air circulation. Sometimes a dog can have two differently shaped ears. You should not probe inside your dog's ears. Only clean that which you can see, *never* delving into the ear canal.

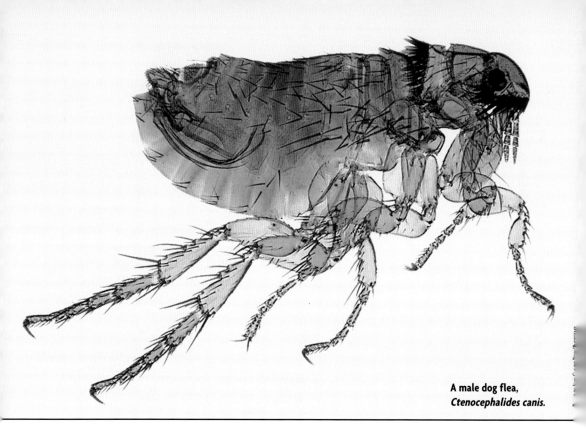

**A male dog flea,**
*Ctenocephalides canis.*

## EXTERNAL PARASITES

### FLEAS

Of all the problems to which dogs are prone, none is more well known and frustrating than fleas. Flea infestation is relatively simple to cure but difficult to prevent. Parasites that are harboured inside the body are a bit more difficult to eradicate but they are easier to control.

To control flea infestation, you have to understand the flea's life cycle. Fleas are often thought of as a summertime problem, but centrally heated homes have changed the patterns and fleas can be found at any time of the year.

The most effective method of flea control is a two-stage approach: one stage to kill the adult fleas, and the other to control the development of pre-adult fleas. Unfortunately, no single active ingredient is effective against all stages of the life cycle.

### LIFE CYCLE STAGES

During its life, a flea will pass through four life stages: egg, larva, pupa and adult. The adult stage is the most visible and irritating stage of the flea life cycle, and this is why the majority of flea-control products concentrate on this stage. The fact is that adult fleas account for only 1% of the total flea population, and the other 99% exist in pre-adult stages, i.e. eggs, larvae and pupae. The pre-adult stages are barely visible to the naked eye.

### THE LIFE CYCLE OF THE FLEA

Eggs are laid on the dog, usually in quantities of about 20 or 30, several times a day. The adult female flea must have a blood meal before each egg-laying session. When first laid, the eggs will cling to the dog's hair, as the eggs are still moist. However, they will quickly dry out and fall from the dog, especially if the dog moves around or scratches. Many eggs will fall off in the dog's favourite area or an area in which he spends a lot of time, such as his bed.

Once the eggs fall from the dog onto the carpet or furniture, they will hatch into larvae. This takes from one to ten days. Larvae are not particularly mobile and will usually travel only a few

S. E. M. BY DR DENNIS KUNKEL, UNIVERSITY OF HAWAII

inches from where they hatch. However, they do have a tendency to move away from light and heavy traffic—under furniture and behind doors are common places to find high quantities of flea larvae.

The flea larvae feed on dead organic matter, including adult flea faeces, until they are ready to change into adult fleas. Fleas will usually remain as larvae for around seven days. After this period, the larvae will pupate into protective pupae. While inside the pupae, the larvae will undergo metamorphosis and change into adult fleas. This can take as little time as a few days, but the adult fleas can remain inside the pupae waiting to hatch for up to two years. The pupae are signalled to hatch by certain stimuli, such as physical pressure—the pupae's being stepped on, heat from an animal's lying on the pupae or

**Magnified head of a dog flea, *Ctenocephalides canis*, colorized for effect.**

### FLEA KILLERS

Flea-killers are poisonous. You should not spray these toxic chemicals on areas of a dog's body that he licks, on his genitals or on his face. Flea killers taken internally are a better answer, but check with your vet in case internal therapy is not advised for your dog.

The dog flea is the most common parasite found on pet dogs.

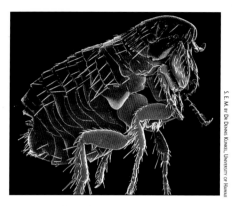

S. E. M. by Dr Dennis Kunkel, University of Hawaii

increased carbon-dioxide levels and vibrations—indicating that a suitable host is available.

Once hatched, the adult flea must feed within a few days. Once the adult flea finds an host, it will not leave voluntarily. It only becomes dislodged by grooming or the host animal's scratching. The adult flea will remain on the host for the duration of its life unless forcibly removed.

Dwight R Kuhn's magnificent action photo, showing a flea jumping from a dog's back.

Photo by Dwight R Kuhn

## Treating the Environment and the Dog

Treating fleas should be a two-pronged attack. First, the environment needs to be treated; this includes carpets and furniture, especially the dog's bedding and areas underneath furniture. The environment should be treated with an household spray containing an Insect Growth Regulator (IGR) and an insecticide to kill the adult fleas. Most IGRs are effective against eggs and larvae; they actually mimic the fleas' own hormones and stop the eggs and larvae from developing into adult fleas. There are currently no treatments available to attack the pupa stage of the life cycle, so the adult insecticide is used to kill the newly hatched adult fleas before they find an host. Most IGRs are active for many months, while adult insecticides are only active for a few days.

When treating with an household spray, it is a good idea to vacuum before applying the product. This stimulates as many pupae as possible to hatch into adult fleas. The vacuum cleaner should also be treated with an insecticide to prevent the eggs and larvae that have been hoovered into the vacuum bag from hatching.

The second stage of treatment is to apply an adult insecticide to

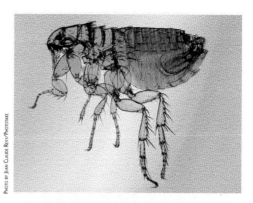

## EN GARDE: CATCHING FLEAS OFF GUARD!

Consider the following ways to arm yourself against fleas:

- Add a small amount of pennyroyal or eucalyptus oil to your dog's bath. These natural remedies repel fleas.
- Supplement your dog's food with fresh garlic (minced or grated) and an hearty amount of brewer's yeast, both of which ward off fleas.
- Use a flea comb on your dog daily. Submerge fleas in a cup of bleach to kill them quickly.
- Confine the dog to only a few rooms to limit the spread of fleas in the home.
- Vacuum daily...and get all of the crevices! Dispose of the bag every few days until the problem is under control.
- Wash your dog's bedding daily. Cover cushions where your dog sleeps with towels, and wash the towels often.

## A LOOK AT FLEAS

Fleas have been around for millions of years and have adapted to changing host animals. They are able to go through a complete life cycle in less than one month or they can extend their lives to almost two years by remaining as pupae or cocoons. They do not need blood or any other food for up to 20 months.

They have been measured as being able to jump 300,000 times and can jump 150 times their length in any direction, including straight up. Those are just a few of the reasons why they are so successful in infesting a dog!

# THE LIFE CYCLE OF THE FLEA

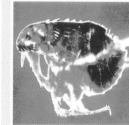

**ggs**　　　**Larvae**　　　**Pupa**　　　**Adult**

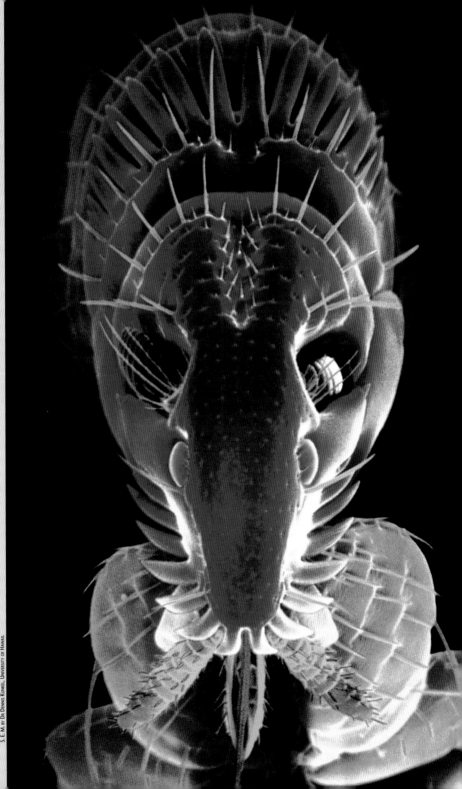

A scanning electron micrograph of a dog or cat flea, *Ctenocephalides,* magnified more than 100x. This image has been colorized for effect.

the dog. Traditionally, this would be in the form of a collar or a spray, but more recent innovations include digestible insecticides that poison the fleas when they ingest the dog's blood. Alternatively, there are drops that, when placed on the back of the animal's neck, spread throughout the fur and skin to kill adult fleas.

## INSECT GROWTH REGULATOR (IGR)

Two types of products should be used when treating fleas—a product to treat the pet and a product to treat the home. Adult fleas represent less than 1% of the flea population. The pre-adult fleas (eggs, larvae and pupae) represent more than 99% of the flea population and are found in the environment; it is in the case of pre-adult fleas that products containing an Insect Growth Regulator (IGR) should be used in the home.

IGRs are a new class of compounds used to prevent the development of insects. They do not kill the insect outright, but instead use the insect's biology against it to stop it from completing its growth. Products that contain methoprene are the world's first and leading IGRs. Used to control fleas and other insects, this type of IGR will stop flea larvae from developing and protect the house for up to seven months.

## DID YOU KNOW?

Never mix flea control products without first consulting your vet. Some products can become toxic when combined with others and can cause fatal consequences.

### TICKS AND MITES

Though not as common as fleas, ticks and mites are found all over the tropical and temperate world. They don't bite, like fleas; they harpoon. They dig their sharp proboscis (nose) into the dog's skin and drink the blood. Their only food and drink is dog's blood. Dogs can get Lyme disease, Rocky Mountain spotted fever (normally found in the US only), paralysis and many other diseases from ticks and mites. They may live where fleas are found and they like to hide in cracks or seams in walls wherever dogs live. They are controlled the same way fleas are controlled.

The dog tick, *Dermacentor variabilis*, may well be the most common dog tick in many geographical areas, especially those areas where the climate is hot and humid. Most dog ticks

A brown dog tick, *Rhipicephalus sanguineus*, is an uncommon but annoying tick found on dogs.

The head of a dog tick, *Dermacentor variabilis*, enlarged and colorized for effect.

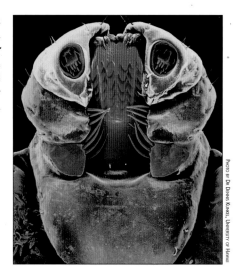

PHOTO BY DR DENNIS KUNKEL, UNIVERSITY OF HAWAII

The great outdoors may be fun for your dog, but it also is an home to dangerous ticks. Deer ticks carry a bacterium known as *Borrelia burgdorferi* and are most active in the autumn and spring. When infections are caught early, penicillin and tetracycline are effective antibiotics, but if left untreated the bacteria may cause neurological, kidney and cardiac problems as well as long-term trouble with walking and painful joints.

S. E. M. BY DR ANDREW SPIELMAN/PHOTOTAKE

have life expectancies of a week to six months, depending upon climatic conditions. They can neither jump nor fly, but they can crawl slowly and can range up to 5 metres (16 feet) to reach a sleeping or unsuspecting dog.

Human lice look like dog lice; the two are closely related.

PHOTO BY DWIGHT R KUHN

### MANGE
Mites cause a skin irritation called mange. Some mites are contagious, like *Cheyletiella*, ear mites, scabies and chiggers. Mites that infest ears are usually controlled with Lindane, which can

only be administered by a vet, followed by Tresaderm at home. It is essential that your dog be treated for mange as quickly as possible because some forms of mange are transmissible to people.

**Opposite page:**
The dog tick, *Dermacentor variabilis*, is probably the most common tick found on dogs. Look at the strength in its eight legs! No wonder it's hard to detach them.

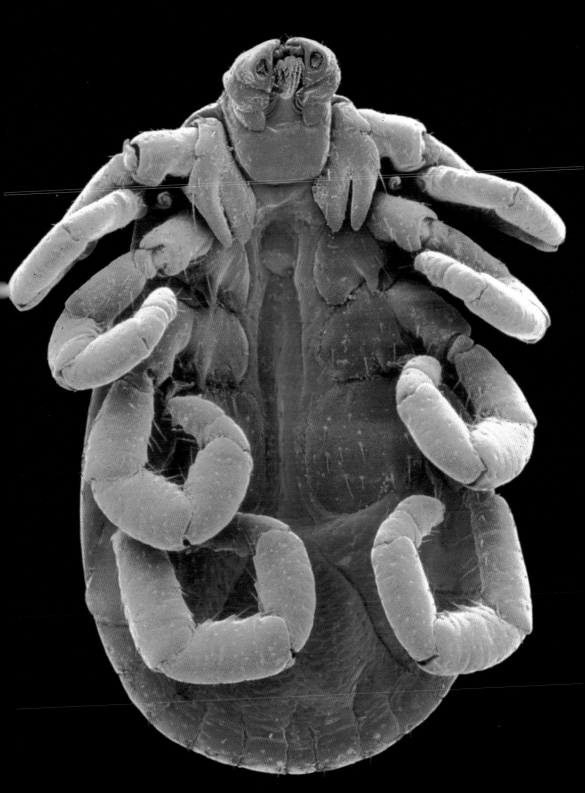

## INTERNAL PARASITES

Most animals—fishes, birds and mammals, including dogs and humans—have worms and other parasites that live inside their bodies. According to Dr Herbert R Axelrod, the fish pathologist, there are two kinds of parasites: dumb and smart. The smart parasites live in peaceful cooperation with their hosts (symbiosis), while the dumb parasites kill their hosts. Most of the worm infections are relatively easy to control. If they are not controlled, they weaken the host dog to the point that other medical problems occur, but they do not kill the host as dumb parasites would.

### ROUNDWORMS

The roundworms that infect dogs are known scientifically as *Toxocara canis*. They live in the dog's intestines. The worms shed eggs continually. It has been estimated that a dog produces about 150 grammes of faeces every day. Each gramme of faeces averages 10,000–12,000 eggs of roundworms. There are no known areas in which dogs roam that do not contain roundworm eggs. The greatest danger of roundworms is

## ROUNDWORMS

Average-size dogs can pass 1,360,000 roundworm eggs every day. For example, if there were only 1 million dogs in the world, the world would be saturated with 1,300 metric tonnes of dog faeces. These faeces would contain 15,000,000,000 roundworm eggs.

Up to 31% of home gardens and children's play boxes in the US contain roundworm eggs.

Flushing dog's faeces down the toilet is not a safe practice because the usual sewage treatments do not destroy roundworm eggs.

Infected puppies start shedding roundworm eggs at 3 weeks of age. They can be infected by their mother's milk.

PHOTO BY CAROLINA BIOLOGICAL SUPPLY/PHOTOTAKE

The roundworm *Rhabditis* can infect both dogs and humans.

that they infect people too! It is wise to have your dog tested regularly for roundworms.

Pigs also have roundworm infections that can be passed to humans and dogs. The typical roundworm parasite is called *Ascaris lumbricoides.*

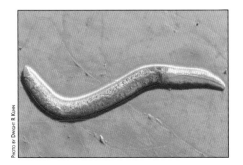

PHOTO BY DWIGHT R KUHN

## DEWORMING

Ridding your puppy of worms is *very important* because certain worms that puppies carry, such as tapeworms and roundworms, can infect humans.

Breeders initiate deworming programmes at or about four weeks of age. The routine is repeated every two or three weeks until the puppy is three months old. The breeder from whom you obtained your puppy should provide you with the complete details of the deworming programme.

Your veterinary surgeon can prescribe and monitor the programme of deworming for you. The usual programme is treating the puppy every 15–20 days until the puppy is positively worm-free. It is advised that you only treat your puppy with drugs that are recommended professionally.

The common roundworm, *Ascaris lumbricoides.*

Left: *Ancylostoma caninum* are uncommonly found in pet or show dogs in Britain.

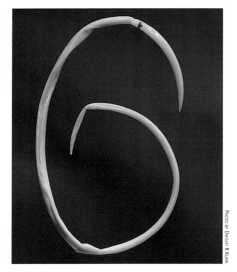

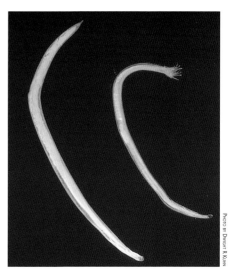

Right: Male and female hookworms.

## HOOKWORMS

The worm *Ancylostoma caninum* is commonly called the dog hookworm. It is also dangerous to humans and cats. It has teeth by which it attaches itself to the intestines of the dog. It changes the site of its attachment about six times a day and the dog loses blood from each detachment, possibly causing iron-deficiency anaemia. Hookworms are easily purged from the dog with many medications. Milbemycin oxime, which also serves as an heartworm preventative in

The infective stage of the hookworm larva.

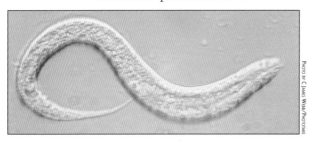

Collies, can be used for this purpose.

In Britain, the 'temperate climate' hookworm (*Uncinaria stenocephala*) is rarely found in pet or show dogs, but can occur in hunting packs, racing Greyhounds and sheepdogs because the worms can be prevalent wherever dogs are exercised regularly on grassland.

## TAPEWORMS

There are many species of tapeworm, all of which are carried by fleas! The dog eats the flea and starts the tapeworm cycle. Humans can also be infected with tapeworms—so don't eat fleas! Fleas are so small that your dog could pass them onto your hands, your plate or your food and thus make it possible for you to ingest a flea that is carrying tapeworm eggs.

## TAPEWORMS

Humans, rats, squirrels, foxes, coyotes, wolves and domestic dogs are all susceptible to tapeworm infection. Except in humans, tapeworms are usually not a fatal infection. Infected individuals can harbour 1000 parasitic worms.

Tapeworms, like some other types of worm, are hermaphroditic, meaning male and female in the same worm.

If dogs eat infected rats or mice, they get the tapeworm disease. One month after attaching to a dog's intestine, the worm starts shedding eggs. These eggs are infective immediately. Infective eggs can live for a few months without an host animal.

While tapeworm infection is not life-threatening in dogs (smart parasite!), it can be the cause of a very serious liver disease for humans. About 50 percent of the humans infected with *Echinococcus multilocularis*, a type of tapeworm that causes alveolar hydatis, perish.

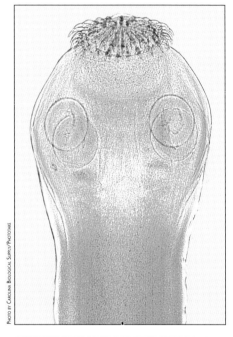

The head and rostellum (the round prominence on the scolex) of a tapeworm, which infects dogs and humans.

PHOTO BY CAROLINA BIOLOGICAL SUPPLY/PHOTOTAKE

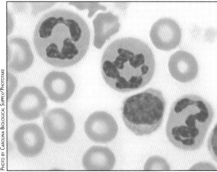

Magnified heartworm larvae, *Dirofilaria immitis*.

PHOTO BY CAROLINA BIOLOGICAL SUPPLY/PHOTOTAKE

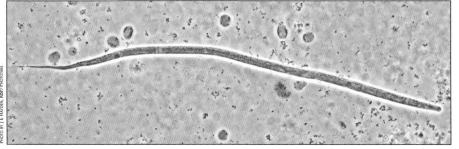

Heartworm, *Dirofilaria immitis*.

PHOTO BY J E HAYDEN, RBP/PHOTOTAKE

# First Aid at a Glance

### Burns
Place the affected area under cool water; use ice if only a small area is burnt.

### Insect bites
Apply ice to relieve swelling; antihistamine dosed properly.

### Animal bites
Clean any bleeding area; apply pressure until bleeding subsides; go to the vet.

### Spider bites
Use cold compress and a pressurised pack to inhibit venom's spreading.

### Antifreeze poisoning
Induce vomiting with hydrogen peroxide. Seek *immediate* veterinary help!

### Fish hooks
Removal best handled by vet; hook must be cut in order to remove.

### Snake bites
Pack ice around bite; contact vet quickly; identify snake for proper antivenin.

### Car accident
Move dog from roadway with blanket; seek veterinary aid.

### Shock
Calm the dog, keep him warm; seek immediate veterinary help.

### Nosebleed
Apply cold compress to the nose; apply pressure to any visible abrasion.

### Bleeding
Apply pressure above the area; treat wound by applying a cotton pack.

### Heat stroke
Submerge dog in cold bath; cool down with fresh air and water; go to the vet.

### Frostbite/Hypothermia
Warm the dog with a warm bath, electric blankets or hot water bottles.

### Abrasions
Clean the wound and wash out thoroughly with fresh water; apply antiseptic.

 *Remember: an injured dog may attempt to bite an helping hand from fear and confusion. Always muzzle the dog before trying to offer assistance.*

## HEARTWORMS

Heartworms are thin, extended worms up to 30 cms (12 ins) long, which live in a dog's heart and the major blood vessels surrounding it. Dogs may have up to 200 worms. Symptoms may be loss of energy, loss of appetite, coughing, the development of a pot belly and anaemia.

Heartworms are transmitted by mosquitoes. The mosquito drinks the blood of an infected dog and takes in larvae with the blood. The larvae, called microfilaria, develop within the body of the mosquito and are passed on to the next dog bitten after the larvae mature. It takes two to three weeks for the larvae to develop to the infective stage within the body of the mosquito. Dogs should be treated at about six weeks of age, and maintained on a prophylactic dose given monthly.

Blood testing for heartworms is not necessarily indicative of how seriously your dog is infected. This is a dangerous disease. Although heartworm is a problem for dogs in America, Australia, Asia and Central Europe, dogs in the United Kingdom are not currently affected by heartworm.

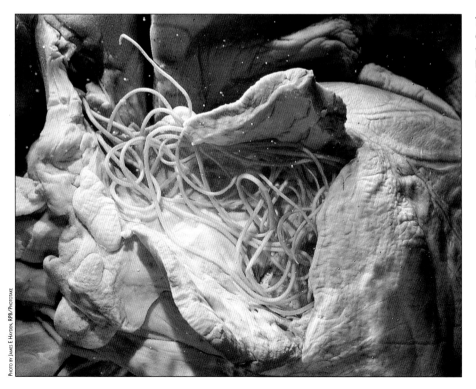

The heart of a dog infected with canine heartworm, *Dirofilaria immitis*.

PHOTO BY JAMES E HAYDEN, RPB/PHOTOTAKE

# HOMEOPATHY:
an alternative
to conventional
medicine

## 'Less is Most'

Using this principle, the strength of an homeopathic remedy is measured by the number of serial dilutions that were undertaken to create it. The greater the number of serial dilutions, the greater the strength of the homeopathic remedy. The potency of a remedy that has been made by making a dilution of 1 part in 100 parts (or 1/100) is 1c or 1cH. If this remedy is subjected to a series of further dilutions, each one being 1/100, a more dilute and stronger remedy is produced. If the remedy is diluted in this way six times, it is called 6c or 6cH. A dilution of 6c is 1 part in 1,000,000,000,000. In general, higher potencies in more frequent doses are better for acute symptoms and lower potencies in more infrequent doses are more useful for chronic, long-standing problems.

## CURING OUR DOGS NATURALLY

Holistic medicine means treating the whole animal as a unique, perfect living being. Generally, holistic treatments do not suppress the symptoms that the body naturally produces, as do most medications prescribed by conventional doctors and vets. Holistic methods seek to cure disease by regaining balance and harmony in the patient's environment. Some of these methods include use of nutritional therapy, herbs, flower essences, aromatherapy, acupuncture, massage, chiropractic and, of course, the most popular holistic approach, homeopathy.

Homeopathy is a theory or system of treating illness with small doses of substances which, if administered in larger quantities, would produce the symptoms that the patient already has. This approach is often described as 'like cures like.' Although modern veterinary medicine is geared toward the 'quick fix,' homeopathy relies on the belief that, given the time, the body is able to heal itself and return to its natural, healthy state.

Choosing a remedy to cure a problem in our dogs is the difficult part of homeopathy. Consult with your veterinary surgeon for a professional diagnosis of your dog's symptoms. Often these symptoms

require immediate conventional care. If your vet is willing, and knowledgeable, you may attempt an homeopathic remedy. Be aware that cortisone prevents homeopathic remedies from working. There are hundreds of possibilities and combinations to cure many problems in dogs, from basic physical problems such as excessive moulting, fleas or other parasites, unattractive doggy odour, bad breath, upset tummy, obesity, dry, oily or dull coat, diarrhoea, ear problems or eye discharge (including tears and dry or mucousy matter), to behavioural abnormalities such as fear of loud noises, habitual licking, poor appetite, excessive barking and various phobias. From alumina to zincum metallicum, the remedies span the planet and the imagination…from flowers and weeds to chemicals, insect droppings, diesel smoke and volcanic ash.

## Using 'Like to Treat Like'

Unlike conventional medicines that suppress symptoms, homeopathic remedies treat illnesses with small doses of substances that, if administered in larger quantities, would produce the symptoms that the patient already has. While the same homeopathic remedy can be used to treat different symptoms in different dogs, here are some interesting remedies and their uses.

### Apis Mellifica
(made from honey bee venom) can be used for allergies or to reduce swelling that occurs in acutely infected kidneys.

### Diesel Smoke
can be used to help control travel sickness.

### Calcarea Fluorica
(made from calcium fluoride, which helps harden bone structure) can be useful in treating hard lumps in tissues.

### Natrum Muriaticum
(made from common salt, sodium chloride) is useful in treating thin, thirsty dogs.

### Nitricum Acidum
(made from nitric acid) is used for symptoms you would expect to see from contact with acids, such as lesions, especially where the skin joins the linings of body orifices or openings such as the lips and nostrils.

### Symphytum
(made from the herb Knitbone, *Symphytum officianale*) is used to encourage bones to heal.

### Urtica Urens
(made from the common stinging nettle) is used in treating painful, irritating rashes.

# HOMEOPATHIC REMEDIES FOR YOUR DOG

| Symptom/Ailment | Possible Remedy |
|---|---|
| **ALLERGIES** | Apis Mellifica 30c, Astacus Fluviatilis 6c, Pulsatilla 30c, Urtica Urens 6c |
| **ALOPAECIA** | Alumina 30c, Lycopodium 30c, Sepia 30c, Thallium 6c |
| **ANAL GLANDS** (BLOCKED) | Hepar Sulphuris Calcareum 30c, Sanicula 6c, Silicea 6c |
| **ARTHRITIS** | Rhus Toxicodendron 6c, Bryonia Alba 6c |
| **CATARACT** | Calcarea Carbonica 6c, Conium Maculatum 6c, Phosphorus 30c, Silicea 30c |
| **CONSTIPATION** | Alumina 6c, Carbo Vegetabilis 30c, Graphites 6c, Nitricum Acidum 30c, Silicea 6c |
| **COUGHING** | Aconitum Napellus 6c, Belladonna 30c, Hyoscyamus Niger 30c, Phosphorus 30c |
| **DIARRHOEA** | Arsenicum Album 30c, Aconitum Napellus 6c, Chamomilla 30c, Mercurius Corrosivus 30c |
| **DRY EYE** | Zincum Metallicum 30c |
| **EAR PROBLEMS** | Aconitum Napellus 30c, Belladonna 30c, Hepar Sulphuris 30c, Tellurium 30c, Psorinum 200c |
| **EYE PROBLEMS** | Borax 6c, Aconitum Napellus 30c, Graphites 6c, Staphysagria 6c, Thuja Occidentalis 30c |
| **GLAUCOMA** | Aconitum Napellus 30c, Apis Mellifica 6c, Phosphorus 30c |
| **HEAT STROKE** | Belladonna 30c, Gelsemium Sempervirens 30c, Sulphur 30c |
| **HICCOUGHS** | Cinchona Deficinalis 6c |
| **HIP DYSPLASIA** | Colocynthis 6c, Rhus Toxicodendron 6c, Bryonia Alba 6c |
| **INCONTINENCE** | Argentum Nitricum 6c, Causticum 30c, Conium Maculatum 30c, Pulsatilla 30c, Sepia 30c |
| **INSECT BITES** | Apis Mellifica 30c, Cantharis 30c, Hypericum Perforatum 6c, Urtica Urens 30c |
| **ITCHING** | Alumina 30c, Arsenicum Album 30c, Carbo Vegetabilis 30c, Hypericum Perforatum 6c, Mezerium 6c, Sulphur 30c |
| **KENNEL COUGH** | Drosera 6c, Ipecacuanha 30c |
| **MASTITIS** | Apis Mellifica 30c, Belladonna 30c, Urtica Urens 1m |
| **PATELLAR LUXATION** | Gelsemium Sempervirens 6c, Rhus Toxicodendron 6c |
| **PENIS PROBLEMS** | Aconitum Napellus 30c, Hepar Sulphuris Calcareum 30c, Pulsatilla 30c, Thuja Occidentalis 6c |
| **PUPPY TEETHING** | Calcarea Carbonica 6c, Chamomilla 6c, Phytolacca 6c |
| **TRAVEL SICKNESS** | Cocculus 6c, Petroleum 6c |

## Recognising a Sick Dog

Unlike colicky babies and cranky children, our canine charges cannot tell us when they are feeling ill. Therefore, there are a number of signs that owners can identify to know that their dogs are not feeling well.

**Take note for physical manifestations such as:**

- unusual, bad odour, including bad breath
- excessive moulting
- wax in the ears, chronic ear irritation
- oily, flaky, dull haircoat
- mucous, tearing or similar discharge in the eyes
- fleas or mites
- mucous in stool, diarrhoea
- sensitivity to petting or handling
- licking at paws, scratching face, etc.

**Keep an eye out for behavioural changes as well including:**

- lethargy, idleness
- lack of patience or general irritability
- lack of appetite, digestive problems
- phobias (fear of people, loud noises, etc.)
- strange behaviour, suspicion, fear
- coprophagia
- more frequent barking
- whimpering, crying

## Get Well Soon

You don't need a DVR or a BVMA to provide good TLC to your sick or recovering dog, but you do need to pay attention to some details that normally wouldn't bother him. The following tips will aid Fido's recovery and get him back on his paws again:

- Keep his space free of irritating smells, like heavy perfumes and air fresheners.
- Rest is the best medicine! Avoid harsh lighting that will prevent your dog from sleeping. Shade him from bright sunlight during the day and dim the lights in the evening.
- Keep the noise level down. Animals are more sensitive to sound when they are sick.
- Be attentive to any necessary temperature adjustments. A dog with a fever needs a cool room and cold liquids. A bitch that is whelping or recovering from surgery will be more comfortable in a warm room, consuming warm liquids and food.
- You wouldn't send a sick child back to school early, so don't rush your dog back into a full routine until he seems absolutely ready.

# Number-One Killer Disease in Dogs: CANCER

In every age, there is a word associated with a disease or plague that causes humans to shudder. In the 21st century, that word is 'cancer.' Just as cancer is the leading cause of death in humans, it claims nearly half the lives of dogs that die from a natural disease as well as half the dogs that die over the age of ten years.

Described as a genetic disease, cancer becomes a greater risk as the dog ages. Veterinary surgeons and dog owners have become increasingly aware of the threat of cancer to dogs. Statistics reveal that one dog in every five will develop cancer, the most common of which is skin cancer. Many cancers, including prostate, ovarian and breast cancer, can be avoided by spaying and neutering our dogs by the age of six months.

Early detection of cancer can save or extend your dog's life, so it is absolutely vital for owners to have their dogs examined by a qualified veterinary surgeon or oncologist immediately upon detection of any abnormality. Certain dietary guidelines have also proven to reduce the onset and spread of cancer. Foods based on fish rather than beef, due to the presence of Omega-3 fatty acids, are recommended. Other amino acids such as glutamine have significant benefits for canines, particularly those breeds that show a greater susceptibility to cancer.

Cancer management and treatments promise hope for future generations of canines. Since the disease is genetic, breeders should never breed a dog whose parents, grandparents and any related siblings have developed cancer. It is difficult to know whether to exclude an otherwise healthy dog from a breeding programme as the disease does not manifest itself until the dog's senior years.

## RECOGNISE CANCER WARNING SIGNS

Since early detection can possibly rescue your dog from becoming a cancer statistic, it is essential for owners to recognise the possible signs and seek the assistance of a qualified professional.

- Abnormal bumps or lumps that continue to grow
- Bleeding or discharge from any body cavity
- Persistent stiffness or lameness
- Recurrent sores or sores that do not heal
- Inappetence
- Breathing difficulties
- Weight loss
- Bad breath or odours
- General malaise and fatigue
- Eating and swallowing problems
- Difficulty urinating and defecating

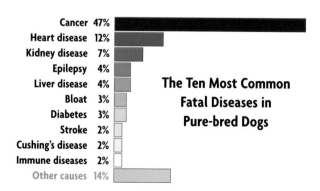

| | |
|---|---|
| Cancer | 47% |
| Heart disease | 12% |
| Kidney disease | 7% |
| Epilepsy | 4% |
| Liver disease | 4% |
| Bloat | 3% |
| Diabetes | 3% |
| Stroke | 2% |
| Cushing's disease | 2% |
| Immune diseases | 2% |
| Other causes | 14% |

**The Ten Most Common Fatal Diseases in Pure-bred Dogs**

Bright clear eyes and a lustrous coat, kept clean and tidy, are indications of your proper care and your dog's good health.

# IRISH RED AND WHITE SETTER

The term *old* is a qualitative term. For dogs, as well as for their masters, old is relative. Certainly we can all distinguish between a puppy Irish Red and White Setter and an adult Irish Red and White Setter—there are the obvious physical traits, such as size, appearance and facial expressions, and personality traits. Puppies and young dogs like to play with children. Children's natural exuberance is a good match for the seemingly endless energy of young dogs. They like to run, jump, chase and retrieve. When dogs grow older and cease their interaction with children, they are often thought of as being too old to keep pace with the children. On the other hand, if an Irish Red and White Setter is only exposed to older people or quieter lifestyles, his life will normally be less active and the decrease in his activity level as he ages will not be as obvious.

If people live to be 100 years old, dogs live to be 20 years old. While this might seem like a good rule of thumb, it is very inaccurate. When trying to compare dog years to human years, you cannot make a generalisation about all dogs. You can make the generali-

sation that most Red and Whites live to be between 10 to 13 years of age.

Most breeds of dog generally are considered physically mature at two to three years of age, but can reproduce even earlier. So, again to generalise, about the first three years of a dog's life are like seven times that of comparable humans. That means a 3-year-old dog is like a 21-year-old human. As the curve of comparison shows, there is no hard and fast rule for comparing dog and human ages. Small breeds tend to live longer than large breeds, some breeds' adolescent periods last longer than others' and some breeds experience rapid periods of growth. The comparison is made even more difficult, for, likewise, not all humans age at the same rate...and human females live longer than human males.

## WHAT TO LOOK FOR IN SENIORS

Most veterinary surgeons and behaviourists use the seven-year mark as the time to consider a dog a 'senior' or 'veteran.' Neither term implies that the dog is geriatric and has begun to fail in mind and body. Ageing is essentially a slowing process. Humans readily admit that they feel a difference in their activity level from age 20 to 30, and then from 30 to 40, etc. By treating the seven-year-old dog as a senior, owners are able to implement certain therapeutic and preventative medical strategies with the help of their veterinary surgeons.

A senior-care programme should include at least two veterinary visits per year and screening sessions to determine the dog's health status, as well as nutritional counselling. Veterinary surgeons determine the senior dog's health status through a blood smear for a complete blood count, serum chemistry profile with electrolytes, urinalysis, blood pressure check, electrocardiogram, ocular tonometry (pressure on the eyeball) and dental prophylaxis.

Such an extensive programme for senior dogs is well advised before owners start to see the obvious physical signs of ageing, such as slower and inhibited movement, greying, increased sleep/nap periods and disinterest in play and other activity. This preventative programme promises a longer, healthier life for the ageing dog. Among the physical problems common in ageing dogs are the loss of sight and hearing, arthritis, kidney and liver failure, diabetes mellitus, heart disease and Cushing's disease (an hormonal disease).

In addition to the physical manifestations discussed, there are some behavioural changes and problems related to ageing dogs. Dogs suffering from hearing or vision loss, dental discomfort or arthritis can become aggressive. Likewise, the near-deaf and/or blind dog may be startled more easily and react in an unexpectedly aggressive manner. Seniors suffering from senility can become more impatient and irritable. Housesoiling accidents are associated with loss of mobility, kidney problems and loss of sphincter control as well as plaque accumulation, physiological brain changes and reactions to medications. Older dogs, just like young puppies, suffer from separation anxiety, which can lead to excessive barking, whining, housesoiling and destructive behaviour. Seniors may become fearful of everyday sounds, such as vacuum cleaners, heaters, thunder and passing traffic. Some dogs have difficulty sleeping, due to discomfort, the need for frequent toilet visits and the like.

Owners should avoid spoiling the older dog with too many fatty treats. Obesity is a common problem in older dogs and subtracts years from their lives. Keep the senior dog as trim as possible, since excessive weight puts additional stress on the

### SENIOR SIGNS

An old dog starts to show one or more of the following symptoms:

- The hair on the face and paws starts to turn grey. The colour breakdown usually starts around the eyes and mouth.

- Sleep patterns are deeper and longer, and the old dog is harder to awaken.

- Food intake diminishes.

- Responses to calls, whistles and other signals are ignored more and more.

- Eye contact does not evoke tail wagging (assuming it once did).

body's vital organs. Some breeders recommend supplementing the diet with foods high in fibre and lower in calories. Adding fresh vegetables and marrow broth to the senior's diet makes a tasty, low-calorie, low-fat supplement. Vets also offer speciality diets for senior dogs that are worth exploring.

Your dog, as he nears his twilight years, needs your patience and good care more than ever. Never punish an older dog for an accident or abnormal behaviour. For all the years of love, protection and companion-ship that your dog has provided, he deserves special attention and courtesies. The older dog may need to relieve himself at 3 a.m. because he can no longer hold it for eight hours. Older dogs may not be able to remain crated for more than two or three hours. It may be time to give up a sofa or chair to your old friend. Although he may not seem as enthusiastic about your attention and petting, he does appreciate the considera-tions you offer as he gets older.

Your Irish Red and White Setter does not understand why his world is slowing down. Owners must make their dogs' transition into their golden years as pleasant and rewarding as possible.

### WHAT TO DO WHEN THE TIME COMES

You are never fully prepared to make a rational decision about putting your dog to sleep. It is very obvious that you love your Irish Red and White Setter or you would not be reading this book.

## NOTICING THE SYMPTOMS

The symptoms listed below are symptoms that gradually appear and become more noticeable. They are not life-threatening; however, the symptoms below are to be taken very seriously and warrant a discussion with your veterinary surgeon:

- Your dog cries and whimpers when he moves, and he stops running completely.

- Convulsions start or become more serious and frequent. The usual convulsion (spasm) is when the dog stiffens and starts to tremble, being unable or unwilling to move. The seizure usually lasts for 5 to 30 minutes.

- Your dog drinks more water and urinates more frequently. Wetting and bowel accidents take place indoors without warning.

- Vomiting becomes more and more frequent.

Putting a beloved dog to sleep is extremely difficult. It is a decision that must be made with your veterinary surgeon. You are usually forced to make the decision when your dog manifests one or more life-threatening symptoms that have become serious enough for you to seek medical (veterinary) help.

If the prognosis of the malady indicates that the end is near and that your beloved pet will only continue to suffer and experience no enjoyment for the balance of its life, then euthanasia is the right choice.

### WHAT IS EUTHANASIA?

Euthanasia derives from the Greek, meaning *good death*. In other words, it means the planned, painless killing of a dog suffering from a painful, incurable condition, or who is so aged that it cannot walk, see, eat or control its excretory functions. Euthanasia is usually accomplished by injection with an overdose of

Your senior setter will cherish moments with his owner as much as ever, though he may seem a little less enthusiastic about showing his appreciation.

anaesthesia or a barbiturate. Aside from the prick of the needle, the experience is usually painless.

## MAKING THE DECISION

The decision to euthanise your dog is never easy. The days during which the dog becomes ill and the end occurs can be unusually stressful for you. If this is your first experience with the death of a loved one, you may need the comfort dictated by your religious beliefs. If you are the head of the family and have children, you should have involved them in the decision of putting your Irish Red and White Setter to sleep. Usually your dog can be maintained on drugs for a few days in order to give you ample time to make a decision. During this time, talking with members of your family or with people who have lived through the same experience can ease the burden of your inevitable decision.

## THE FINAL RESTING PLACE

Dogs can have some of the same privileges as humans. The remains of your beloved dog can be buried in a pet cemetery, which is generally expensive. Alternatively, your dog can be cremated individually and the ashes returned to you. A less expensive option is mass cremation, although, of course, the ashes cannot then be returned. Vets can usually arrange the cremation on your behalf. The cost of these options should always be discussed frankly and openly with your veterinary surgeon. In Britain, if your dog has died at the surgery, the vet legally cannot allow you to take your dog's body home, as home garden burials are not permitted.

## GETTING ANOTHER DOG?

The grief of losing your beloved dog will be as lasting as the grief of losing a human friend or relative. In most cases, if your dog died of old age (if there is such a thing), it had slowed down considerably. Do you want a new Irish Red and White Setter puppy to replace it? Or are you better off finding a more mature Irish Red and White Setter, say two to three years of age, which will usually be house-trained and will have an already developed personality? In this case, you can find out if you like each other after a few hours of being together.

The decision is, of course, your own. Do you want another Irish Red and White Setter or perhaps a different breed so as to avoid comparison with your beloved friend? Most people usually buy the same breed because they know (and love) the characteristics of that breed. Then, too, they often know people who have the same breed and perhaps they are lucky enough that one of their friends expects a litter soon.

# IRISH RED AND WHITE SETTER

When you purchase your Irish Red and White Setter, you will make it clear to the breeder whether you want one just as a loveable companion and pet, or if you hope to be buying an Irish Red and White Setter with show prospects. No reputable breeder will sell you a young puppy and tell you that it is *definitely* of show quality, for so much can go wrong during the early months of a puppy's development. If you plan to show, what you will hopefully have acquired is a puppy with 'show potential.'

To the novice, exhibiting an Irish Red and White Setter in the show ring may look easy, but it takes a lot of hard work and devotion to do top winning at a show such as the prestigious Crufts Dog Show, not to mention a little luck too!

The first concept that the canine novice learns when watching a dog show is that each dog first competes against members of its own breed. Once the judge has selected the best member of each breed (Best of Breed), provided that the show is judged on a Group system, that chosen dog will compete with other dogs in its group. Finally, the best of each group will compete for Best in Show and Reserve Best in Show.

The second concept that you must understand is that the dogs are not actually compared against one another. The judge compares each dog against its breed standard, which is a written description of the ideal specimen of the breed. While some early breed standards were indeed based on specific dogs that were famous or popular, many dedicated enthusiasts say that a perfect specimen, as described in the standard, has never walked into a show ring, has never been bred and, to the woe of dog breeders around the globe, does not exist. Breeders attempt to get as close to this ideal as possible with every litter, but theoretically the 'perfect' dog is so elusive that it is impossible. (And if the 'perfect' dog were born, breeders and judges would never agree that it was indeed 'perfect.')

If you are interested in exploring the world of dog showing, your best bet is to join your local breed club. These clubs often host both Championship

### HOW TO ENTER A DOG SHOW

To enter a dog show in Britain, you need to look at one of the two dog papers, which come out on Fridays and can be ordered at any newsagent. Find the phone number of the secretary of a show, and call to obtain a schedule and entry form. Fill in the form with the classes you wish to enter (double-check your form!) and do not forget to send a cheque for the entries. Show entries close six weeks or so before the show.

You cannot enter the show if your dog is not registered with The Kennel Club. If you have sent off the forms to The Kennel Club to transfer the dog into your name, it is possible to enter with 'TAF' (transfer applied for) after the dog's name.

training days and seminars in order that people may learn more about their chosen breed. To locate the breed club closest to you, contact The Kennel Club, the ruling body for the British dog world. The Kennel Club governs not only conformation shows but also working trials, obedience shows, agility trials and field trials. The Kennel Club furnishes the rules and regulations for all of these events plus general dog registration and other basic requirements of dog ownership. Its annual show, called the Crufts Dog Show, held in Birmingham, is the largest benched show in England. Every year over 20,000 of the UK's best dogs qualify to participate in this marvellous show, which lasts four days.

The Kennel Club governs many different kinds of shows in Great Britain, Australia, South Africa and beyond. At the most competitive and prestigious of these shows, the Championship Shows, a dog can earn Challenge Certificates (CCs), and thereby become a Show Champion or a Champion. The CCs necessary to

and Open Shows, and sometimes Match meetings and special events, all of which could be of interest, even if you are only an onlooker. Clubs also send out newsletters, and some organise

### KC RECOGNITION

The Kennel Club of Great Britain recognised the Irish Red and White Setter as a separate breed in 1979, and the following year the first breed representative was entered at Crufts.

make up a Show Champion may be earned only at Championship Shows. A Challenge Certificate is awarded to each Best of Sex winner at shows where CCs are offered. A dog must win three CCs under three different judges in order to earn the Show Champion (Sh Ch) title. If he accomplishes this feat before he is one year old, he must win another CC after that time before the title is awarded. As a slower-maturing breed, few Irish Red and White Setters become Show Champions in this manner.

CCs are awarded to a very small percentage of the dogs competing, and dogs that are already Champions compete with others for these coveted CCs. The number of CCs awarded in any one year is based upon the total number of dogs in each breed entered for competition.

Some breeds must also qualify in a field trial in order to gain the title of full Champion, and the Irish Red and White Setter is one such breed. To become a full Champion (Ch), the Irish Red and White must prove his ability in the field by earning a Certificate of Merit (CM) or a placement at a field trial, or by gaining a Show Gundog Working Certificate in a field test.

To become an Irish Show Champion in his native land, an Irish Red and White Setter must earn 40 Green Star points, including four Majors of at least five points each. Points are determined by the number of dogs entered in the show. An Irish Show Champion title requires a field qualification as well.

**TYPES OF CONFORMATION SHOWS**
There are three types of Championship Shows: an all-breed General Championship Show for all Kennel-Club-recognised breeds; a Group Championship Show, which is limited to breeds within one of the groups; and a Breed Show, which is usually confined to a single breed. The Kennel Club determines which breeds at which Championship Shows will have the opportunity to earn Challenge Certificates (or tickets). Serious exhibitors often will opt not to participate if the tickets are withheld at a particular show. This policy makes earning championships even more difficult to accomplish.

Open Shows are generally less competitive and are frequently used as 'practice shows' for young dogs. There are hundreds of Open Shows each year, all of which can be delightful social events and are great first-show experiences for the novice. Even if you're consid-ering just watching a show to wet your paws, an Open Show is a great choice.

The World Dog Show for the new millennium took place in Milan, Italy and attracted thousands of dogs and handlers from around the world.

While Championship and Open Shows are most important for the beginner to understand, there are other types of shows in which the interested dog owner can participate. Training clubs sponsor Matches that can be entered on the day of the show for a nominal fee. In these introductory-level exhibitions, two dogs' names are pulled out of an hat and 'matched,' the winner of that match goes on to the next round and eventually only one dog is left undefeated.

Exemption Shows are much more light-hearted affairs with usually only four pedigree classes and several 'fun' classes, all of which can be entered on the day of the show. Exemption Shows are sometimes held in conjunction with small agricultural shows and the proceeds must be given to a charity. Limited Shows are also available in small number. Entry is restricted to members of the club that hosts the show, although one can usually join the club when making an entry.

Virtually all countries with a recognised speciality breed club (sometimes called a 'parent' club) offer show conformation competition specifically for and among Irish Red and White Setters. Under direction of the club, other special events for hunting, tracking, obedience and agility may be offered as well, whether for titling or just for fun.

**OTHER TYPES OF COMPETITION**
Irish Red and White Setters are eligible to enter Pointer and Setter trials. A properly bred dog should be most capable of mastering the qualifying tests to become certified in the field. In Ireland, setters participate more often in field trials than in Great Britain. One sees more and more Red and Whites at agility trials, but less often at obedience competitions.

## SHOW RING BASICS

There is much more to showing and winning with a dog than trotting about the ring with your lovely dog at the end of a show lead. The dog's physical fitness and attributes, coat condition, proper grooming and gait, as well as the handler's composure and attire, all contribute to success in the show ring. Irish Red and White Setter owners interested in bench competition should align themselves with other show fanciers to acquaint themselves with the rules and finer points of this canine activity.

Before you actually step into the ring, you would be well advised to sit back and observe the judge's ring procedure. If it is your first time in the ring, do not be over-anxious and run to the front of the line. It is much better to stand back and study how the exhibitor in front of you is performing. The judge asks each handler to 'stand' the dog, hopefully showing the dog off to his best advantage. The judge will observe the dog from a distance and from different angles, and approach the dog to check his teeth, overall structure, alertness and muscle tone, as well as consider how well the dog 'conforms' to the standard. Most importantly, the judge will have the exhibitor move the dog around the ring in some pattern that he or she should specify. Finally, the judge will give the dog one last look before moving on to the next exhibitor.

If you are not in the top three at your first show, do not be discouraged. Be patient and consistent, and you may eventually find yourself in the winning line-up. Remember that the winners were once in your shoes and have devoted many hours and much money to earn the placement. If you find that your dog is losing every time and never getting a nod, it may be time to consider a different dog sport or to just enjoy your Irish Red and White Setter as a pet.

## FIELD TRIALS

The title of Field Trial Champion (FT Ch) is the most difficult of titles, and only one Irish Red and White Setter has achieved that lofty status. A dog must win two first prizes in the Open Stake under two different judges at two different field trial competitions for Setters and Pointers, or win the separate Setter and Pointer Championship Stake.

Few Irish Red and White Setters today compete successfully in field trials. In Ireland, it is more common for dogs to earn a CM, and, as of the year 2000, ten Red and Whites had accomplished that. Many more attempt to gain a qualifying certificate, which is offered at a non-competitive field event. In Great Britain, more and more breeders and handlers are attracted to conformation showing rather than to field events.

## WORKING TRIALS

Working trials can be entered by any well-trained dog of any breed, not just Gundogs or Working dogs. Many dogs that earn the Kennel Club Good Citizen Dog award choose to participate in a working trial. There are five stakes at both Open and Championship levels: Companion Dog (CD), Utility Dog (UD), Working Dog (WD), Tracking Dog (TD) and Patrol Dog (PD). As in conformation shows, dogs compete against a standard and, if the dog reaches the qualifying mark, it obtains a certificate.

The exercises are divided into groups, and the dog must achieve at least 70 percent of the allotted score for each exercise in order to qualify. If the dog achieves 80 percent in the Open level, it receives a Certificate of Merit (CM); in the Championship level, it receives a Qualifying Certificate. At the CD stake, dogs must participate in four groups: Control, Stay, Agility and Search (Retrieve and Nosework). At the next three levels, UD, WD and TD, there are only three groups: Control, Agility and Nosework.

The Agility exercises consist of three jumps: a vertical scale up a six-foot wall of planks; a clear jump over a basic three-foot hurdle with a removable top bar; and a long jump across angled planks stretching nine feet.

To earn the UD, WD and TD, dogs must track approximately one-half mile for articles laid from one-half hour to three hours previously. Tracks consist of turns and legs, and fresh ground is used for each participant. The fifth stake, PD, involves teaching manwork, which is not recommended for every breed.

## AGILITY TRIALS

Agility trials began in the United Kingdom in 1977 and have since spread around the world, especially to the United States, where they are very popular. The handler directs his dog over an obstacle course that includes jumps (such as those used in the working trials), as well as tyres, the dog walk, weave poles, pipe tunnels, collapsed tunnels, etc. The very enthusiastic Irish Red and White Setter is a natural for this high-energy and challenging sport. Spectators thrill to watch the athletic setter joyfully racing about the agility course with typical Irish grace and glee.

The Kennel Club requires that dogs not be trained for agility until they are 12 months old. This dog sport is great fun for dog and owner, and interested owners should join a training club that has obstacles and experienced agility handlers who can introduce you and your dog to the 'ropes' (and tyres, tunnels, etc.).

## FÉDÉRATION CYNOLOGIQUE INTERNATIONALE

Established in 1911, the Fédération Cynologique Internationale (FCI) represents the 'world kennel club.' This international body brings uniformity to the breeding, judging and showing of pure-bred dogs. Although the FCI originally included only five European nations: France, Germany, Austria, the Netherlands and Belgium (which remains its headquarters), the organisation today embraces nations on six continents and recognises well over 300 breeds of pure-bred dog.

The FCI sponsors both national and international shows. The hosting country determines the judging system and breed standards are always based on the breed's country of origin. Dogs from every country can participate in these impressive canine spectacles, the largest of which is the World Dog Show, hosted in a different country each year.

There are three titles attainable through the FCI: the *International Champion*, which is the most prestigious; the *International Beauty Champion*, which is based on aptitude certificates in different countries; and the *International Trial Champion*, which is based on achievement in obedience trials in different countries.

The top award in an FCI show is the CAC (*Certificat d'Aptitude au Championnat*) and to gain a championship, a dog must win three CACs at regional or club shows under three different judges who are breed specialists. The title of International Champion is gained by winning four CACIBs (*Certificats d'Aptitude au Championnat International de Beauté*), which are offered only at international shows, with at least a one-year lapse between the first and fourth award.

The FCI breeds are divided into ten groups. At the World

Standing for inspection, the Red and White's conformation is displayed to its best advantage as dog and handler await evaluation by the judge.

Dog Show, the following classes are offered for each breed: Puppy Class (6–9 months), Junior Class (9–18 months), Open Class (15 months or older) and Champion Class. A dog can be awarded a classification of Excellent, Very Good, Good, Sufficient and Not Sufficient. Puppies can be awarded classifications of Very Promising, Promising or Not Promising. Four placements are made in each class. After all classes are judged, a Best of Breed is selected. Other special groups and classes may also be shown. Each exhibitor showing a dog receives a written evaluation from the judge.

Besides the World Dog Show and other all-breed shows, you can exhibit your dog at speciality shows held by different breed clubs. Speciality shows may have their own regulations.

# INDEX

# My Irish Red and White Setter

PUT YOUR PUPPY'S FIRST PICTURE HERE

Dog's Name _____

Date _____ Photographer _____